Emily Brontë's
Wuthering Heights

Adapted for the stage by
Charles Vance

Samuel French – London
New York – Sydney – Toronto – Hollywood

WUTHERING HEIGHTS

First presented by Prestige Plays on a national tour, which opened at the Grand Opera House, Belfast, on 20th February, 1989 with the following cast, in order of appearance:

Mr Lockwood   Dermot Walsh
Tenant of Thrushcross Grange
Joseph   Mike Shannon
Manservant at Wuthering Heights
Cathy Linton   Joanna Steele
Daughter of Catherine and Edgar
Linton, widow of Linton Heathcliffe
Hareton Earnshaw   Mark Alexander
Son of Hindley Earnshaw
Heathcliff   John Blakey
Ellen Dean   Vivienne Moore
Housekeeper of Thrushcross Grange
Catherine Earnshaw   Lynn Clayton
of Wuthering Heights
Edgar Linton   Ian Oliver
of Thrushcross Grange
Hindley Earnshaw   Martin Head
Catherine's elder brother
Isabella Linton   Jane Bullman
Edgar's younger sister

Directed by **Charles Vance**
Designed by **Stephen Howell**
Lighting by **Peter Hunter**

The play was presented in association with Salisbury Playhouse and the British Theatre Association

The action of the play takes place in Wuthering Heights and Thrushcross Grange and spans several years. Period: early Victorian

Notes on the production of Wuthering Heights
By the adapter who directed the first production

To encapsulate an epic novel into something less than $2\frac{1}{2}$ hours theatre entertainment requires major cuts in the original text and the inevitable 'narration' to bridge the spans of time and to take account of characters in the original novel who do not appear in the play.

I attempted to achieve this both in the adaption and in my first production by maintaining the dialogue between Ellen Dean and Lockwood which opens the second scene of the play and reminding my audience that the performance from then until the last scene of the play was in a form of flashback. To avoid that tiresome convention of the narrator addressing the audience, throughout the play at appropriate times and in shadowy light the character of Lockwood, still in his dressing gown, would appear as though watching the play unfold as Ellen narrates the story of Heathcliff and Cathy to him. In this way, each time one of her narrative pieces is due to begin, Lockwood is there and with appropriate changes of light she is able to address those comments to him and so keep continuity from that second scene of the play in Thrushcross Grange.

In this way, therefore, by the penultimate scene of the play, we are still in Thrushcross Grange with Ellen Dean telling Lockwood the story and the end of the play unfolds 'in the present'.

For simple continuity, it is desirable to keep a composite set of Wuthering Heights on stage right and Thrushcross Grange on stage left, with the centre area between the two as common ground for each of the sets. That same common ground can be used for those scenes of soliloquy when Cathy or Heathcliff are 'pin-spotted' away from either of the two houses.

This composite set gives us the opportunity scenically to delineate the dramatic difference between the gaunt, stark Wuthering Heights, epitomising all that is bleak on the West Yorkshire moors, and the delicate elegance of Thrushcross Grange, a typical home of the gentry.

The dramatic changes between these scenes and indeed between the emotional tirades of the two protagonists can be achieved by simple, yet subtle and dramatic lighting changes.

It is a challenging story and makes for exciting theatre and I hope that each director who tackles the play will enjoy creating his own images and not feel bound by the conventions within which I have created the adaptation.

Charles Vance

ACT I

The CURTAIN rises on a completely dark stage. Music. Wind howling fiercely around

Lockwood, muffled, stands in a pinspot

Lockwood Imagine you are a lonely traveller
Lost on a winter day,
Lost among these bleak, northern hills: moorland country.
You are trudging towards a house,
Set high on a crag:
It is evening,
A light glimmers:
There surely will be shelter for the night!

A sorrowful sight!
Dark night coming down early
Sky and hills mingle in one bitter swirl
Of wind and suffocating snow.

You would turn back if you knew where you were going!
You would seek the stinking lair of the fox
Or the rocky cavern inhabited by the wolf
Rather than dare that threshold!
But you are innocent of these things and press on.
Toil the granite track towards the gate;
Even the pandemonium of dogs ahead seems sweet encouragement!
Across the yard to the great door and the ancient bell:
You do not have to wake the dead with your desperate call
The restless dead and the bitter living mingle freely here
In this place exposed to great winds and tempests
In this place of unquiet spirits:
Wuthering Heights!

Lockwood exits

The Lights creep up on the gloomy kitchen of Wuthering Heights. Cathy is crouched in the fireplace, almost invisible

The bell rings. Then, to loud knocking and the bedlam of dogs, Joseph, an ancient man-servant, moves across the stage

Joseph The Lord help us! All reet—all reet, I'm coming. Quiet, you curs!

He goes off. There is the sound of a door being opened—chains, bolts, etc.

What the devil is the matter?

He enters with Lockwood

Lockwood What the devil indeed! The herd of possessed swine could have had no worse spirits in them than those animals of yours, sir! You might as well expose a stranger to a brood of tigers!

Joseph They'll none meddle with them as touch nowt! The dogs do reet to watch and guard—and ye'll do well to leave 'em alone. Yon's not pets! Who are y' anyroad? What are ye for?

Lockwood Mr Lockwood. The new tenant of Thrushcross Grange across the valley. I'm here to pay my respects to Mr Heathcliff, my landlord.

Joseph 'T' maister's down in t' fold. Go back road y' come an' down by t' end o' t' barn if ye want to talk wi' 'im.

Joseph moves as if to go

Lockwood Is there nobody else?

Joseph is already in the gloom

There must be . . . (*After a pause, calling*) Is there anyone there? Anyone at home?

Joseph (*returning*) There's none but t' missis . . . and she'll not bother wi' ye though y' make yer flaysome din all neet.

Lockwood Call her!

Joseph Not me! I'll have no hand in it! If y' want her, she's yon . . .

He nods towards a far corner of the fire enclosure where Cathy sits crouched over the blaze. Her dress, once good, shows signs, like her hair and person, of neglect. Her manner alternates between a sullen listlessness and quick anger at the slightest provocation

Joseph exits

Lockwood advances and begins in a conversational tone:

Lockwood Rough weather! I am afraid, Mrs Heathcliff, the noise is the consequence of your servant's leisurely attendance. I had hard work to make myself heard.

Silence

She regards him as if from a distance, looks him up and down as though she isn't sure if he is really there; then suddenly:

Cathy Were you asked to tea?

Lockwood I should be glad to have a cup.

Cathy Were you asked?

Lockwood (*smiling*) No. You are the proper person to ask me.

Hareton appears. He is a strong, well-built youth, his bearing 'free, almost haughty' and at odds with his appearance, which is that of a farm labourer—but he shows none of the domestic's attitudes. He is struggling into some sort of rough upper garment

Cathy (*to Lockwood*) You are not required to teach me manners. Don't you know where you are? Manners—quiet speech—such things have been forgotten, long forgotten in this house.

She tries to reach a cannister on the mantel which is rather too high for her

Hareton speaks from a distance without looking at Lockwood

Hareton If it's Mr Heathcliff you're seeking, you'll like as not find him in the dairy—
through there.
Lockwood Thank you. Very well—with your permission I will attempt to find him—
(*He is about to go, then turns to Cathy*) Allow me to help you—
Cathy I don't want your help. I can manage myself.
Lockwood I beg your pardon. The dairy?

*He moves away, but does not know which way to go. He stands awkwardly in the
shadows*

Cathy has reached again for the cannister

Hareton quietly comes to her side and is about to get it for her when she turns to him

Cathy Get away this instant!
Hareton Cathy!
Cathy How dare you touch me—you're filthy and vile and you stink!
Hareton Cathy!
Cathy Get away—you know I can't endure you!
Hareton Cathy, what could I have done?
Cathy Come near me and I'll go back upstairs and never come down again!
Hareton How am I to blame?
Cathy Just by coming near me! That's how you are to blame.
Hareton You've been upstairs so long. I was glad to see you down. I thought now
you are better—we might be friends—
Cathy *Friends!*
Hareton At night I'm stalled wi' havin' naught to do. When the lamp is lit and the
work is done, I should like to hear you read—
Cathy Because you cannot, Dunce!
Hareton I could like to hear you read to me from one of your books.
Cathy *Mister* Earnshaw—and the whole pack of you—just be good enough to
understand that I reject any pretence of kindness any of you have the hypocrisy to
offer. I will have nothing to do with any of you. I despise you.
Hareton But what have *I* done?
Cathy When I would have given my life for one kind word, even to see one of your
faces, you all kept off. Why should I bother to complain to you though? I am driven
down here by the cold, not to amuse you or enjoy your company.
Hareton Whatever cause you might have to be angered—and I reckon you have
some—it's not my doin' and I'm not in any way to blame ...
Cathy (*sarcastically*) No! *You're* the exception! I've never missed the concern of a
clod like you.
Hareton When you was sick—after—after Linton was dead ... I offered ... I offered
more than once. I asked Mr Heathcliff to let me wake for you ...
Cathy Be silent! One word more and I'll go. I'll go anywhere—? Outside into the
snow, anywhere rather than have your disagreeable voice in my ear.
Hareton (*angrily moving away*) You can go to hell for me! That's what you can do! I'll
have nowt more to do wi' you. Stop upstairs—go out— go to hell!

Joseph enters

Joseph We're in for a reet do wi' this lot! Roads'll be covered in half-an-hour.
(*Looking around*) Where's that fella ... (*He sees Lockwood in the shadows*) Ah—
there you are! Y've got summat in front of ye gettin' to the Grange in this!
Lockwood Then I must ask ...
Joseph Ask me nowt! Anythin' you've got to ask, ask t'maister an' see what sort of a
reply ye'll get! I reckon y' can do it now an' all 'cos 'e's comin''–eh! Tha'd better
shift thyself, missis!

A very dim light allows us to see Heathcliff descending the stairs at the back

Lockwood Mr Heathcliff?

Heathcliff nods

Mr Lockwood, your new tenant, sir—

Heathcliff gives no response

Lockwood, uncomfortable, assumes an air of false cheerfulness

You see, sir—I am come according to promise! I fear I shall be weatherbound for
half-an-hour, perhaps you would be good enough to afford me shelter during that
time?
Heathcliff Half-an-hour?
Lockwood Well ...
Heathcliff I wonder you choose the thick of a snowstorm to ramble about the
country, sir? Don't you know you run the risk of being lost in the marshes?
Lockwood I must admit the severity of the weather, coming as suddenly as it did,
surprises me. But if I wait a while—surely—
Heathcliff There is no chance of a change.
Lockwood Perhaps I can get a guide amongst your lads? He could stop over at the
Grange until morning. Could you spare me one?
Heathcliff No I could not.
Lockwood Then I shall have to make the attempt—trust to my own account.
Heathcliff Ha!
Joseph (*to Cathy*) Are you for makin' t' tea missis?
Cathy (*to Heathcliff, nodding at Lockwood*) Is he to have any?
Heathcliff (*snapping savagely*) Get it ready!
Lockwood (*trying to ease the situation*) This house of yours is quite remarkable, Mr
Heathcliff. On my next visit, I must get you to tell me something of its history.
Indeed, over the door I detected that it was completed in fifteen hundred ...
"Wuthering" I understand is a local adjective descriptive of the atmospheric tumult
to which its station is exposed—

*Cathy continues to prepare tea by the hearth. Joseph has moved into the shadows.
Hareton has found himself a hunk of bread which he breaks and eats and a basin into
which he presently receives his tea. Heathcliff stands moodily gazing into the fire. None
of them pays the slightest attention to Lockwood who continues his attempt at polite
conversation*

It is strange, strange how custom can mould our tastes and ideas. Many could not
imagine the existence of happiness in a life of such complete exile from the world as
you spend, Mr Heathcliff ...

Heathcliff turns and regards him balefully

And yet—I'll venture to say that, surrounded by your family, and with your amiable lady as the presiding genius over your home and heart . . .

Heathcliff My amiable lady! Where is she—my amiable lady?

Lockwood I beg your pardon. I have committed a blunder—I should have realised— from the disparity in your ages—(*He takes tea from Cathy*) Oh, thank you, ma'am.

He tries to cover his embarrassment by drinking his tea, his eye meanwhile on Heathcliff who now maliciously tempts him into further indiscretion

Heathcliff (*lightly*) Mrs Heathcliff is my daughter-in-law.

Hareton is raising a basin of tea to his lips

Lockwood Ah, certainly, now I understand (*to Hareton*) *You* are the favoured possessor of the beneficent fairy?

Hareton springs up, clenching his fists in fury

Hareton By God!

Heathcliff Unhappy in both your conjectures! We neither of us have the privilege of owning your good fairy. *Her mate is dead.* I said she was my daughter-in-law, therefore she must have married my son . . .

Lockwood And this young man is—

Heathcliff Most assuredly *not* my son!

Hareton My name is Hareton Earnshaw and I'd counsel you to respect it!

Lockwood I meant—and intended no disrespect, believe me—

He rises and makes for the door in confusion

Thank you for the tea, it was very welcome—I bid you—

Lockwood exits and immediately returns

Good heavens! This is terrible! I don't think it is possible for me to get home without a guide. The roads will be buried already!

Heathcliff Hareton, drive those dozen sheep into the barn porch. They'll be covered if left in the fold all night. And put a plank before them.

Hareton goes out

Heathcliff exits

Lockwood How must I do?

There is no response

After a moment Cathy returns the cannister with difficulty to the mantel and stands gazing at the fire

Joseph appears behind Lockwood, speaking to Cathy

Joseph As wonder 'ow' y' can fashion to stand there i' idleness when all of 'em is goin' about—

Lockwood How do you mean sir—?

Joseph (*ignoring him and continuing to Cathy*) But y'r a nowt an' it's no use talkin'. Ye'll never mend y'r ill ways but go reet to t' devil, like y'r mother afore ye.

Cathy You scandalous old hypocrite! Do you dare mention the devil's name to me? Aren't you afraid you'll be carried away bodily?

Joseph Why you—

Cathy I warn you—stop provoking me, or I'll ask your abduction as a special favour.

Joseph Damned witch—

Cathy takes a large book from the fireplace

Cathy Look, Joseph! I'll show you how far I have progressed in the Black Art! I'll soon be competent to make a clear house of it! The old cow didn't die by chance. And as for your rheumatism—

Joseph Oh wicked! Wicked! Lord God above deliver us from evil!

Cathy Too late, reprobate! You're lost—a castaway! Now be off, or I'll hurt you seriously. I've got you all modelled in wax, and the first who passes the limits I fix shall—I'll not say what shall be done to him—but you'll see—you'll see! Go! I'm looking at you!

Joseph backs out muttering

Joseph (*as he goes*) Wicked—wicked slut . . .

Joseph exits

Lockwood Mrs Heathcliff, you must excuse me for troubling you—I am sure you are at heart truly very kind—Do point out some landmarks by which I may find my way home. I have no more idea of how to get there than you would have of how to get to London!

Cathy Take the road you came (*She sits by the fire and reads*)

Lockwood But my dear Mrs Heathcliff . . .

Cathy It is brief advice but as sound as I can offer.

Lockwood But if you hear of me being discovered dead in a bog or a drift of snow, will not your conscience whisper that it is partly your fault?

Cathy How so? I cannot escort you.

Lockwood You! I should be sorry to think I should ask you!

Cathy They wouldn't let me go so far as the garden gate, any time—never mind the weather—

Lockwood I want you to *tell* me the way.

Cathy How? You wouldn't find it on an ordinary dark night.

Lockwood Then persuade Mr Heathcliff to give me a guide.

Cathy Who?

Lockwood Well—anyone suitable.

Cathy There's himself, Hareton, Joseph and me. Which would you have?

Lockwood Are there no boys?

Cathy No. Those are all.

Lockwood Then it follows that I am compelled to stay.

Cathy That you may settle with your host; I have nothing to do with it.

Heathcliff enters followed by Hareton

Heathcliff I hope this will be a lesson to you to make no more rash journeys in these hills.

Lockwood You may be assured of that!

Heathcliff As for staying here—I don't keep accommodation for visitors.
Lockwood Any sort of bed will do.
Heathcliff Any bedfellow? Would you prefer Joseph or Hareton?
Lockwood Really now . . .
Heathcliff You share a bed with one or the other if you stay.
Lockwood A chair in this room will do.
Heathcliff Oh no! A stranger is a stranger. It doesn't suit me to permit anyone the range of the place while I'm off guard!
Lockwood This is insufferable!
Hareton I'll go wi' him as far as the park.
Heathcliff You'll go with him to hell!
Hareton How else will he manage?
Heathcliff And who's to look after the horses?
Cathy A man's life is of more consequence than horses. Somebody must go.
Heathcliff Not at your bidding! And see here—if you set any store by him, you'd best be quiet.
Cathy Oh, I'll be quiet—let him go then, let him be lost! And I hope his ghost will haunt you! I hope you never get another tenant until the Grange is in ruins! (*She flings herself in the far corner of the settle*)

Joseph appears with a lighted storm-lantern

Joseph 'Arken, 'arken to t' witch cussin' t' maister now . . .

Lockwood, on impulse, snatches the lantern from Joseph and runs off. We hear the door crash open and an immediate uproar from the dogs

Maister, maister, he's stealin' t'lantern! Hey, Gnashter! Hey, dog! Hey, Wolf! Hold him! Hold him!

Hareton goes to Lockwood's rescue and brings him back slightly the worse for wear

Lockwood By God, sir, you should be called to account for keeping such beasts!
Heathcliff Not bitten are you?
Lockwood If I had been I'd have set my signet on the biter.
Heathcliff (*with a rare, if somewhat sardonic grin*) Come, come, you are flurried, Mr Lockwood. Here, take a little wine—
Lockwood Thank you, no.
Heathcliff Guests are so rare here that I and my dogs hardly know how to receive them, this I am willing to own. A glass of wine?
Lockwood No thank you.
Heathcliff (*to Hareton*) Find him somewhere above. Take him away.

Hareton and Lockwood go off up the stairs. Lockwood waits on the landing

(*To Joseph*) In the morning see him on his way as soon after dawn as work permits.

He turns to Cathy, who is still at the end of the settle and who has picked up the book and is reading

As for you, you worthless bitch—the rest one way or another earn their bread; you live on my charity! Put your trash away and find something to do!
Cathy I will put my trash away because you can make me if I refuse . . .

Heathcliff And I will ...
Cathy You needn't tell me what you are capable of.
Heathcliff Quiet!
Cathy So I obey. (*She flings the book on the settle*) For the rest, you shall not master me. You forced me here, forced me to marry your son against my will—(*She runs to the stairs and speaks over the rail*) now I am your responsibility—but I will do nothing, though you swear your tongue out, nothing but what I please!
Heathcliff You will do one thing for certain: one way or another you will pay me for having you eternally in my sight! Now get out! Go to bed, go to the devil or where you will, but out of my sight—
Cathy I know the weight of your hand—I'll go. But inside—here—I'm my own mistress still.
Heathcliff GO!

Cathy exits

Heathcliff picks up her book from the settle and hurls it after her up the stairs. He stands staring after her for a moment then goes to the settle and sits, as though spent, with his head against the back and his eyes closed

The Lights fade until the scene is dark

A low moan of wind. Somewhere a clock chimes a quarter hour

The Lights trap down to Heathcliff, who takes a lighted candle and stands listening

Time is as meaningless here as my life. For me there is not time of any worth except this, in the middle of the night when I move about the house listening and waiting. A hundred times a night I open and close my eyes. I choose this hour because it is the quietest on the clock: the night is over, the day is not begun. The sleepers sleep or restlessly anticipate the shudder of rising. No one about except myself! Even the prowling fox, after a bloody forage through the pens, has dragged his prey back to a bone-filled earth. The house creaks, it is not yet time for the earliest to stir. Now ... Cathy! Cathy!

From above there is a sudden frenzied cry of fright

(*Starting in terror*) Who is that?

A slight pause. Lights up slightly

Lockwood comes running down the stairs

Who is that?
Lockwood It is only I.
Heathcliff God confound you Lockwood! God damn you man—
Lockwood I was awakened by the most frightful nightmare.

Lockwood comes down to the fire

Heathcliff (*crossing to him and putting the candle down*) Where have you been? Where have you just come from?

Lockwood does not reply

Heathcliff regards him for a second then rushes off up the stairs, returning in a moment in great rage

Who put you in that room *and in that bed?* Who? I'll turn them out of the house this instant ... *who?*

Lockwood I'm damned if I know or care, that girl—your daughter-in-law; throw her out if you will, she deserves it. I suppose she wanted to get another proof that the place was haunted at my expense.

Heathcliff Did you say ...

Lockwood "Haunted"—swarming with ghosts and goblins. You have reason for shutting that room up, believe me.

Heathcliff My reasons are my own concern.

Lockwood I'll not go back. I'll walk the yard till daylight. I'll not endure again the persecutions of your ancestors.

Heathcliff What do you mean?

Lockwood Why, if the little fiend had got in, she would have strangled me.

Heathcliff What are you saying?

Lockwood Wicked little soul—she deserves to walk the earth for twenty years!

Heathcliff Twenty years—

Lockwood Suddenly I was awakened by—a fierce tapping on the window. It was the branch of a fir tree, rattling its cones against the panes, as the blast wailed by. For an instant I listened doubtingly, then turned and dozed—and dreamt. Again the noise. This time I did not wake— at least, I hope I didn't—

Heathcliff What happened?

Lockwood Again I heard the gusty wind, again the driving of the snow—then again that devil's tattoo. It annoyed me so much I resolved to silence it. I struggled with the casement catch, to open it and break off the branch, but found the hook was soldered to the staple—"I must stop it nevertheless," I muttered, and knocked my fingers through the glass—no blood, you see! I stretched my arm through the hole to reach the branch, and my fingers closed—on the fingers of a hand!

Heathcliff shrinks back

A little ice-cold hand—that grasped mine and would not let it go. The intense horror of nightmare came over me. I tried to draw back my arm but still the hand clung to it. And a most melancholy voice sobbed out: "Let me in! Let me in!" And still it clung on. "Let me in!" it cried, "I'm come home. I'd lost my way on the moor." Through the window I discerned dimly a child's face. Terror made me cruel. And, finding I could not shake the creature off, I pulled its wrist onto the broken pane, and rubbed it to and fro till the blood ran down and soaked the bedclothes. And still it clung on and cried, "Let me in!"—almost maddening me with fear. "How can I?" cried I. "Let me go, if you want me to let you in." The fingers relaxed. I snatched mine through the hole, piled a pyramid of books against it and stopped my ears to keep out the lament. "Be gone!" I cried "I'll never let you in, not if you beg for twenty years!" "It *is* twenty years," mourned the voice, "I've wandered the moors for twenty years." There was a feeble scratching and the pile of books began to move. I tried to jump up, but could not. "Who are you?" I cried.

Heathcliff No!

Lockwood "I'm Catherine," it replied.

Heathcliff No!

Lockwood "Catherine Linton."

Heathcliff What can you mean by talking this way to me? How dare you—how dare you, under my roof!—God, you risk your life to speak to me so! (*He falls back, struggling to vanquish his violent emotion*)

Lockwood (*calming*) The truth is, I fancy, less melodramatic—I recall that I spent the first part of the night gazing around the room, then spelling out the name scratched again and again on the window-sill—'Catherine Linton"—"Catherine—". A monotonous occupation, calculated to send me to sleep—(*He looks at his watch*) Not three o'clock yet! Time stagnates here—we must surely have retired at eight.

Heathcliff Nine in winter, rise at four. (*He turns to Lockwood*) Mr Lockwood, you may go to my room for the remainder of the night. You'll only be in the way down here, and your cry has sent sleep to the devil for me.

Lockwood For me too. I'll stay down here till daylight, and then be off. And you need not fear a repetition of my intrusion. I am now quite cured of seeking pleasure in society.

Heathcliff Then go where you please. I shall join you directly. Keep out of the yard, though—the dogs are unchained. Go, though you only wander about the steps and passages. I'll come in two minutes. Away with you!

Lockwood takes the candle, and moves slowly away. On his way out he looks back at Heathcliff

The Lights trap down

Heathcliff looks about him

> Come in! Come in!
> Cathy, do come, oh do come—*once* more!
> Oh, my heart's true love, hear me *this* time—
> Come, at last!
> Catherine! . . .

A breeze blows. The Lights fade, then come up on Ellen Dean in the corner of the other side of the stage. For a moment she stands, then moves to her chair where she sits and takes up her sewing

Ellen The clock was chiming twelve when Mr Lockwood came through the door of Thrushcross Grange next morning. How he made his way home through those snow-drifts is more than I can fathom—we had quite given him up for lost, and were preparing to search for his remains. A terrible state he was in too! He slept all afternoon by his study fire—he prefers his own company—but when I took his supper in, he asked me to stay. "You've lived here a considerable time haven't you?" he says. "Didn't you say sixteen years?" "Eighteen sir," I says, "I came when the mistress was married, to wait on her, and after she died, the master retained me as housekeeper." Ah times are greatly changed since then!

Lockwood enters wearing a smoking-jacket and slippers. He sits by Ellen

Lockwood You've seen a great many alterations, I suppose.

Ellen I have—and trouble too. I beg your pardon for asking, but how did you find young Mrs Heathcliff?

Lockwood Well, I suppose, and handsome. But not, I think very happy.

Ellen Oh dear, I don't wonder!
Lockwood Heathcliff had a son, it seems—this girl is his widow?
Ellen Yes, sir. She is the daughter of my late master and mistress, Edgar Linton and Catherine—
Lockwood Catherine Linton!
Ellen Catherine Earnshaw that was.
Lockwood Catherine *Earnshaw*?
Ellen The name is familiar to you, sir?
Lockwood Then you came with her from Wuthering Heights?
Ellen Yes, sir. You seem surprised?
Lockwood And you have long known Heathcliff?
Ellen Aye. How did you like him sir?
Lockwood A rough character, I would say, Mrs Dean.
Ellen Rough as a saw-edge. Hard as whin-stone! The less you meddle with him the better!
Lockwood He must have had some ups and downs to make him so. What's his history?
Ellen A cuckoo's sir. A foundling, picked up on the streets of Liverpool, when he was no more than six, by Catherine's father, old Mr Earnshaw—the last true master of Wuthering Heights—Hindley, her older brother, resented and hated Heathcliff from the day he was brought home. Whereas Catherine and Heathcliff—
Lockwood Why did they call him Heathcliff?
Ellen It was the name of a son who died in infancy—and it has served him ever since, both for Christian and surname. As soon as old Earnshaw died, Hindley gave Heathcliff a dog's life. He stopped his lessons and banished him to the lowest duties of the yard and field. Yet Heathcliff stood his blows and complained so seldom that I really thought him not vindictive. Worse was in store when Hindley's wife died in childbirth—
Lockwood A son—Hareton Earnshaw?
Ellen Aye—my first bonny nursling. But Hindley blamed him for his wife's death— and gave himself up to drink and the devil. The servants could not bear his tyrannical ways—Joseph and I were the only two who would stay—
Lockwood And Catherine?
Ellen Catherine and Heathcliff were inseparable. The greatest punishment I could invent was to keep her from him. Hindley drove them ever closer together. Day after day they would run away to the moors, like two young animals, and not come home till evening. I've cried to myself to watch them growing more reckless. Joseph might thrash Heathcliff till his arm ached—they forgot everything the moment they were together again. It was only when they ran here to Thrushcross Grange— and Catherine met Edgar Linton that things began to change. . . .

Daylight builds in the room at Wuthering Heights

Catherine Earnshaw, a dark girl in her teens, runs in, trying on what is apparently her best silk dress

Catherine (*calls*) Nelly! Nelly, come here! Hurry!

Ellen crosses to her

It's all wrong. And they'll be here soon! I'll look a sight against Isabella, but what can you expect? These are the clothes that were bought for me when I stayed over at the Grange—Isabella will have had half a dozen frocks since then.

Ellen (*fussing around her*) You'll look very well indeed. You're not exactly going to a royal ball—keep still—Mr Edgar and Miss Isabella are spoilt in the way of clothes and playthings if you ask me. Now let me see—you're fit enough to go anywhere but we must do something with your hair.

Catherine My hair's all right, leave it alone. What's the matter with it?

Ellen Well you might ask! You can't expect to look like a lady—like Miss Isabella— and behave half your time like a tomboy, running off over the moors with Heathcliff on every occasion that offers.

Catherine I'll not give him up. No matter what you say and in spite of Hindley I'll not give him up.

Ellen Nobody's asking you to.

Catherine Yes, you are! You know as well as I do that Hindley hates me being with him, but then Hindley hates everything—even his own baby.

Ellen Don't say things like that—

Catherine And don't pull my hair! Leave it alone. I'll finish it myself. Edgar will be here soon.

Ellen Very ladylike I'm sure—quite the queen of the countryside! But let me tell you, you'll never grow up and take your place in the society of the district until you pay heed to your elders—I don't hold with the way Hindley treats Heathcliff myself, but I agree with him that you must be stopped from copying his gypsy vagabond ways.

Catherine Heathcliff is not a vagabond! He is as good as you or I—or Hindley—and worth a dozen simpering Edgar Lintons.

Ellen Look, miss, don't come your pert ways with me, or master or no master, I'll fetch you the slap you're asking for!

Catherine You just dare!

Ellen If Mr Hindley were in now . . .

Catherine Well he's not in, is he? He's out, thank God. I want the place to myself.

Ellen Miss Catherine!

Catherine (*mimicking*) "Miss Catherine"! I hate being me—I'll tear this frock . . . I'll . . .

Ellen Do as you please but do it alone. You'll be in a better temper, miss, before I'll have any truck with you.

Ellen goes out

Catherine unsuccessfully attempts to complete her toilet

Heathcliff comes in

Catherine is much put out to see him. She seizes a book and sits reading

Heathcliff Cathy, are you going anywhere?

Catherine No.

Heathcliff Oh. I wondered.

Catherine It looks like rain. What did you wonder?

Heathcliff Oh, nothing.

Catherine It didn't take you much effort then, did it?

Heathcliff Why are you so bad-tempered?

Catherine How do you know whether I'm bad-tempered or not?

Heathcliff I can tell. You wouldn't be reading that book upside down if you were interested in it.

Catherine (*closing the book with a bang*) You should be in the field now. It's an hour past dinner-time. I thought you had gone. (*After a slight pause*) Heathcliff, did you hear me?

Heathcliff I'll not work any more today. Yes, I heard you. I said "I'll not work any more today".

Catherine My, aren't we grand all of a sudden?

Heathcliff Hindley doesn't often free us from his damnable presence—so I'll not work. I'll stay here with you.

Catherine Joseph will tell.

Heathcliff Joseph is loading lime on the other side of Pennistone Crag.

Catherine Oh. Of course. I thought I hadn't seen him.

Heathcliff It will take him till dark.

Catherine I suppose it will.

Heathcliff So he'll never know! (*He makes himself comfortable with a book*) Even though Hindley stopped me taking lessons I can still read—I expect I know nearly as much as you—except Latin of course. (*After a short pause*) I know what we will do!

Catherine What?

Heathcliff You said you weren't going out—didn't you?

Catherine Yes.

Heathcliff Nobody coming here, is there?

Catherine Not that I know of.

Heathcliff Why have you got your silk dress on then?

Catherine I often change in the afternoon. Don't you notice?

Heathcliff How can I when I'm working like a ploughboy in the fields? I don't change my clothes from one week's end to the other if you've ever noticed. (*Pause*) Shall I get cleaned up now?

Catherine You can if you like—(*A pause. Casually*) Isabella and Edgar Linton talked of calling this afternoon ... as it's on the point of raining I hardly expect them but—

Heathcliff But what?

Catherine Well, they might tell—accidentally of course—of you being here—you don't want to risk Hindley finding out for nothing—

Heathcliff Oh Cathy! Order Nelly to say that you are engaged—

Catherine Nelly and I are out of sorts; she wouldn't do it.

Heathcliff So you're going to turn me out?

Catherine Well ...

Heathcliff Turn me out for these pitiful, silly friends of yours! Sometimes I almost feel like telling you—telling you—but I'll not—

Catherine Telling me what? Tell me! Go on—go on or I'll shake it out of you!

Heathcliff Nothing.

Catherine Nothing? That's no answer. Tell me what?

Heathcliff (*jumping up and tearing a calendar from the wall*) Look at this calendar! The crosses are for the evenings you have spent with the Lintons; the dots for those you have spent with me. Do you see? I've marked every day.

Catherine Yes, I see. Very foolish.
Heathcliff Why foolish?
Catherine As if I took notice. Where's the sense in it? Why do you do it?
Heathcliff To show you I *do* take notice.
Catherine So I should always be sitting with you? What good do I get? What do you talk about? You might be dumb or a baby for anything you say to amuse me, or for anything you do, for that matter.

Hooves are heard on the flags outside

Heathcliff Cathy! You never told me before that I talked too little—or you disliked my company.
Catherine It's no company to be with people who know nothing and say nothing!

Heathcliff is about to retort but, hearing footsteps, strides angrily out
Ellen comes in, glances at the fire and then starts dusting around the place
Suddenly young Edgar Linton comes in gaily and with a bright smile

Edgar In spite of the dark clouds, it's a wonderful day! Isabella asks to be excused— she was afraid it would rain and didn't fancy the ride—so I left early on my own—
Catherine (*seeing Ellen*) In the nick of time I would say. What are you doing there, Nelly?
Ellen My work, miss.
Edgar You're looking splendid, Catherine. I can't believe we are going to have the place to ourselves.

Catherine drops him a slightly ironic curtsy

Ellen (*aside*) Little does he know!
Edgar Come ... (*He takes Catherine by the hand*)
Catherine Delighted to be at your service, sir.
Edgar You have the sunniest disposition—you will be a great asset to me in my social life!
Ellen (*aside*) You should see her in bare feet and a dirty shift tumbling in the barn with Heathcliff!
Catherine Your social life, Edgar? Lord, I cannot see myself gracing that to any effect.
Edgar No young lady of my acquaintance has more natural talent; I hope you are studying to improve your accomplishments—
Ellen You can say that again!
Catherine I can never compete with Isabella, nor, I think you will agree, have I the opportunity to do so.
Edgar You will forgive me saying so, but considering the nature of your environment, you emerge with credit. Which reminds me—Isabella and my mother think it is high time you paid us an extended stay at the Grange.
Ellen And give us a well-deserved holiday at the Heights!
Catherine I will speak to my brother, Hindley—there is nothing I would like more. I am glad you appreciate how I have to struggle against the limitations of my rustic condition—
Edgar As a rose struggles to emerge from thorns ...

Ellen nearly chokes

Catherine Poor Nelly, you work too hard. (*She dances over to Ellen during this and arriving at her side hisses in her ear*) Take yourself and your dusters off—when I have company, servants retire! (*Aloud*) Don't bother any more, Nelly. You may go.

Ellen Oh no, miss. It's a good opportunity to catch up while the master is away. He hates me to be fidgeting in his presence. I'm sure Mr Edgar will excuse me.

Edgar (*too well bred to demur*) You may be sure I understand, Mrs Dean.

Catherine I'd hate you to be fidgeting in *my* presence! (*Dropping the pretence*) Take yourself off!

Ellen Now, miss, mind your company!

Catherine You disobey me?

Ellen I am sorry for it, miss—I have other orders to consider.

Catherine Edgar—amuse yourself—go on watching the clouds—pay no attention to our little domestic difficulties—

Edgar Indeed, the clouds are heavy—it looks like a storm. (*Aside*) In more ways than one!

Catherine Nelly, you and I will have words later—

Ellen I am quite content it should be later, miss—

Catherine snatches the duster from Ellen's hand and pinches her arm spitefully. Ellen starts up

Oh! Miss! That was a nasty trick! I am not going to bear it!

Catherine (*flaring up*) I didn't touch you, you lying creature!

Ellen (*to Catherine and also to Edgar*) What's that then? (*She exhibits the mark*)

Catherine (*stamping*) Whatever it is, let it join that! (*She slaps her face hard, and shakes her*)

Edgar (*interposing*) Catherine! Love . . . Catherine . . .

He tries to lead Catherine away. She wheels round and slaps him even harder

Catherine Take that, you ninny—now go on, cry, I expect you still can.

Edgar assumes great dignity and goes straight to his hat, takes it, and proceeds to the door

Ellen That's right! Take warning and begone!—Now you know what she is really like.

Catherine Where are you going? You must not go!

Edgar I must and shall!

Catherine No! Not yet, Edgar Linton! You shall not leave me in that mood. I should be miserable all night and I won't be miserable for you!

Edgar How can I stay after you have struck me?

Catherine is silent

You have made me afraid and ashamed of you. I'll not come here again.

Catherine (*beginning to cry*) Edgar . . . please . . .

Edgar And you told a deliberate untruth!

Catherine I didn't! I did nothing deliberately! Well, go if you want—go, go, go! Get away! And now I'll cry. (*She falls to her knees by a chair*) I'll cry myself sick!. (*She bursts into tears*)

Edgar hovers irresolutely. Ellen comes between them

Ellen Miss is dreadfully wayward, sir! As bad as any spoiled child.

Catherine sets herself to weep in earnest

Harken to her! You'd best be riding home, sir, or she will work herself into a paddy and a passion, and make herself sick only to grieve us.

Edgar looks back at Catherine

Ellen turns towards Lockwood who is watching in the shadows

The soft thing had no more power to depart, than a cat to leave a mouse it has caught.

Edgar moves to Catherine and puts his arm about her to comfort her

Edgar Catherine. Catherine. My love, don't cry like that—it upsets me. Hush Catherine, only I am to blame, listen to me—hush.

He kisses her. She calms down

Edgar leads Catherine off. The lights check down

Ellen There would be no saving him. Doomed. Flown to his fate! (*She attends to the fire*)

Ellen goes off and we hear the door being bolted. She returns, sets a cradle by the fire and sits gently rocking it

Now then Hareton my love? Peacefully asleep? Thou art the only one in all the household who knows content. (*She gently rocks the cradle*)

Heathcliff comes in

Heathcliff Where is Edgar Linton?
Ellen Away any time now I should hope. He knows well enough Master Hindley is due.
Heathcliff I would like to break his bloody back.
Ellen That will do! You blame your condition on others but you do nothing to help yourself. You were forbidden the Grange years ago for that kind of talk. Do you know what old Mrs Linton called you?
Heathcliff What I called her was more likely the truth!
Ellen "Nasty swearing gipsy-boy"—that's what she called you.
Heathcliff Fat-arsed old besom!
Ellen You must change your manners—*and* your appearance if you wish to keep Miss Catherine for a friend.
Heathcliff Aye. Well ... I'll think about it. Sometimes I have a mind to improve myself ... so that I may do ... all I intend.
Ellen Unless you do you'll lose Miss Catherine for sure—she is getting used to the ways of gentlefolk.
Heathcliff Much good may it do her! (*Pause*) What should I do to make myself decent, Nelly?
Ellen That's more like it! (*She takes up Catherine's mirror*) Here, come to the glass and I'll tell you what you should wish. Wish and learn to smooth away that surly frown like a vicious dog which expects all the world to kick it—Look at the world boldly. Smile now and then.

Heathcliff In other words I must wish for Edgar Linton's bright blue eyes and baby forehead?

Ellen Well—

Heathcliff If I do—it won't help me to get them.

Ellen A good *heart* will help you to a bonny face, my lad.

Heathcliff So you think I *may* do?

Ellen Have a look in the mirror again and tell me if you can see what I see—

Heathcliff I can only see what I have always seen.

Ellen Are you sure? Tell me, don't you think yourself rather handsome?

Heathcliff Stop plaguing me, Nelly.

Ellen I tell you, I do. Has no one ever told you you look fit for a prince in disguise?

Heathcliff All anyone has ever told me is that—I am a gypsy brat, picked off the street of Liverpool when I was six. What could be lower than that?

Ellen Pay no heed to what anyone says. Who knows? Who knows but that your father was Emperor of China and your mother an Indian queen? Each of them able to buy up Wuthering Heights and Thrushcross Grange on one week's wages.

Heathcliff Who knows but one day *I* will. Without them.

Ellen You were kidnapped by wicked sailors and brought to England! Were I in your place I would frame high notions of my birth and the thoughts of what I was should give me courage and dignity to bear the oppressions of a little farmer like Hindley Earnshaw!

Heathcliff It would be very odd if you were right—

Ellen You see—I'll be proud of you yet.

Heathcliff If you live long enough you might change your mind. You'd change it now if you knew what I was thinking!

Ellen I've told you, you must give up such thoughts.

Heathcliff I am trying to settle how I shall pay Hindley back—when I'm thinking of that, I don't feel pain—I don't care how long I wait if only I can do it at last. All I hope is that he doesn't die before I do!

Ellen Hush!

Heathcliff I'll give him a blow for every one he's given me. I'll reduce him to the beggar he tries to make of me! By the living God I'll make him curse the day he was born—and if I can see him die in misery and all his offspring suffer I'll be satisfied— but only then will I be satisfied.

Ellen God will punish you for such wicked thoughts. Do you realize you are cursing the innocent baby in the cradle?

Heathcliff If I had my way I'd take him and his father, smash their skulls and paint the house-front with their blood!

Ellen For shame!

A crash off stage

Heathcliff I think I hear the swine!

Ellen Oh dear! We must have Hareton out of the way—what am I to do? (*Realizing there is no time to remove the baby she pushes the cradle into the shadows*) Heathcliff! Don't go!

Hindley Earnshaw enters. He is very drunk

Hindley (*overhearing Ellen and imitating her*) "Heathcliff, don't go!" What are you doing in here, you son of a gypsy's bitch?

Ellen Nay sir—

Hindley sees the mirror

Hindley What's this? (*He grabs Heathcliff and looks him up and down, eventually flinging him away*) What's this? Attempting the coxcomb? A bit of boot and whip will soon alter that. (*He cuts hard at Heathcliff with his whip*)

Heathcliff moves into the shadows

Ellen Now, sir, Heathcliff is here at my bidding. He is in no wise in the wrong and should not be treated so.

Hindley (*turning on Ellen and grabbing her*) You feeling frisky are you? Where's Hareton—you're always putting him out of my way. Tell me! I wonder how far you could take a carving knife down your throat without squawking?

Ellen Now, sir, none of your games tonight! I'm not in the mood.

Hindley Not in the mood, you bitch? There. (*He pulls her by the skin of her neck like a dog*) Where have you hidden my son?

Ellen Come, sir—enough. (*She is afraid of him and tries to humour him*) Come along now—

Hindley I have murder in me tonight. I'll do for you Nelly—you needn't laugh!

Ellen There is a fire in your room—

Hindley I'll kill someone—I shall have no rest till I do!

Ellen And the bed is warm—

Hindley I'm not ready for bed. I *want my son*. Where is he?

Ellen Where he is safe from you I hope.

Hindley Where is he?!

Ellen I'll not let you handle him, until you are yourself.

Hindley When I'm myself I don't want to handle him as you damn well know. Now where is he? (*He thrusts her away*) Where's my son? HARETON! Come to thy father, damn thee! (*He searches about and is on the point of giving up when he stumbles over the cradle*) Ah! Hareton, I have found thee out! (*He takes the bundle from the cradle and holds it high in the air*)

Ellen watches in terror

I have found thee out Hareton! What sort of a monster is this? (*He shakes the baby*)

Ellen tries to get it from him

Ellen Nay, sir—

Hindley (*holding it from him*) By God, as if I would breed such a monster!

Ellen Help!

Hindley I'll break the brat's neck!

He runs up the stairs, holding the baby high. Ellen follows

Ellen Help—Heathcliff!

Heathcliff moves from the shadows

Hindley (*turning suddenly*) What the—

Hindley leans too far over and drops the baby. By a natural impulse Heathcliff catches the child as it falls. Ellen rushes down and takes it from him. He looks her straight in the eye

Heathcliff I have to wait it seems.

Hindley (*sobered and abashed; coming down*) It's your fault Ellen—You should have kept him out of sight. You should have taken him from me. Is he injured?

Ellen (*in tears of relief*) Injured! If he's not killed he'll be an idiot. You're worse than a heathen, treating your own flesh and blood in that manner!

Hindley Let me see—

Ellen You shall not meddle with him! He hates you—they all hate you! A happy family you have—and a pretty state you are come to!

Heathcliff (*moving to the dresser*) I shall come to a prettier yet, Nelly! I'm not the devil's own yet by a long way! Take yourself and the boy away. And, hark you, Heathcliff—clear out of my reach and hearing—(*he produces a brandy bottle*)

Ellen What are you about, sir?

Hindley (*ignoring her; addressing Heathcliff*) Go on—get out. I won't murder you tonight—unless I set the house on fire—but that's as my fancy goes—(*He pours and drinks*)

Ellen Nay, don't! Mr Hindley, take warning. Have mercy on this unfortunate boy if you care nothing for yourself!

Hindley Anyone will do better for him than I shall.

Ellen Have mercy on your own soul!

Hindley (*taking the bottle and again mounting the stairs*) Not I! On the contrary, I shall have great pleasure in sending it to Hell to punish its maker! (*He drinks as he goes off*) Here's to a hearty damnation!

Hindley exits

Ellen What are we to do? God will surely punish him! (*She fusses about the baby in the cradle*)

Heathcliff God will not have the satisfaction that I will.

Ellen (*to the baby*) Thy father's a pretty one, isn't he lad?

Catherine enters

Heathcliff moves into the shadows behind the settle

Catherine Nelly! Where's Heathcliff?

Ellen (*coldly*) About his work in the stable, I should think.

Catherine Good. I don't want to see him just now.

Ellen (*after a pause*) Well, miss? Have you anything to say for this afternoon's behaviour?

Catherine Oh that! It's all part of the same thing.

Ellen Indeed? And you call that an explanation?

Catherine It's part of not wanting Heathcliff about. If you promise not to scold me I'll tell you about it.

Ellen I think it's high time you were in bed.

Catherine Oh, Nelly! I am so very unhappy!

Ellen A pity. You're hard to please—so many friends and so few cares and can't make yourself content!

Catherine Nelly . . . you're not cross with me still? All right, I'm sorry. Truly sorry for being such a pig. Am I forgiven?

Ellen I will think about it.

Catherine I want you to do something for me.

Ellen Ah-ah . . . I thought there was a catch in it!

Catherine No, you don't. I am not going to ask you to do something—well, not *do* something—I want you to keep a secret for me.

Ellen (*indifferently*) Oh.

Catherine Will you?

Ellen Is it worth keeping?

Catherine Yes. And it worries me, and I must let it out! I want to know what I should do. I've no one else at all to go to with this . . . will you keep my secret?

Ellen I've told you. If it's worth keeping.

Catherine Edgar Linton has just asked me to marry him.

Ellen And it's to be a secret?

Catherine Well, yes, but that's not it—that's not the secret I mean. I've given him an answer—

Ellen makes a face

No . . . now listen. Before I tell you whether it was "yes" or "no", I want *you* to tell *me* which it ought to have been!

Ellen Really Miss Catherine, how can I know?

Catherine Think hard for a minute, then tell me.

Ellen Considering the exhibition you performed in Mr Edgar's presence this afternoon, I might say it would be wise to refuse him. Since he asked you *after* that, he must be either hopelessly stupid or a venturesome fool.

Catherine (*moving away*) If you talk so I won't tell you any more. (*Pause*) I accepted him, Nelly. Be quick and say whether I was wrong.

Ellen You accepted him!

Catherine Yes, yes! Now, tell me!

Ellen What's the use of talking about it? You have pledged your word.

Catherine Was I wrong?

Ellen Right or wrong, you can't retract.

Catherine But say whether I should have done so! Do!

Ellen There are many things to be considered before that question can be answered.

Catherine (*in despair*) Oh . . .

Ellen First and foremost, do you love Mr Edgar?

Catherine Who can help loving Edgar Linton? Of course I do.

Ellen Why do you love him, Miss Cathy?

Catherine Nonsense, I do. That's enough.

Ellen By no means. You must say how.

Catherine Well, because he is handsome and pleasant to be with.

Ellen Bad!

Catherine And because he is young and cheerful.

Ellen Bad still.

Catherine And because he loves me.

Ellen Bad, coming there.

Catherine And he will be rich! I shall enjoy being mistress of the Grange and the greatest woman in the neighbourhood.
Ellen Worst of all! Now say *how* you love him.
Catherine As everybody loves—oh, don't be silly, Nelly.
Ellen Not at all. Answer!
Catherine I love the ground under his feet, and the air over his head, and everything he touches, and every word he says—I love all his looks, and all his actions, and him entirely and altogether. There now!
Ellen And why?
Catherine No. Now you are making a jest of it. It is no jest to me!
Ellen I am very far from jesting, Miss Catherine. Your reasons are not enough. There are several other handsome, rich young men in the world. What should hinder you from loving them?
Catherine They are out of my way. I've seen none like Edgar.
Ellen You may! And he won't always be handsome and young—he may not always be rich.
Catherine He is now. I have only to do with the present.
Ellen Well, that settles it. If you have only to do with the present, marry Mr Linton!
Catherine I do not need your permission for that! I *shall* marry him. You still have not told me whether I'm right.
Ellen Perfectly right, if people be right to marry only for the present. So let us hear what you are unhappy about. Hindley will be pleased. Old Mr and Mrs Linton will not object I think. You will escape from a disorderly, comfortless home into a wealthy, respectable one. You love Edgar, Edgar loves you. All seems smooth and easy. Where is the obstacle?
Catherine (*striking her head and breast*) *Here*! And *here*! In which ever place the *soul* lives. In my soul and in my heart I know, I know I'm wrong!
Ellen How very strange.
Catherine *That* is my secret! *That* is what I wanted to whisper to you. Mock me and I'll go no further, listen and I'll explain it. I can't do it distinctly, but I'll give you a feeling of how I feel. If I were in heaven, Nelly, I should be extremely miserable.
Ellen That's because you are not fit to go there.
Catherine It's not for that. I dreamt once that I was there.
Ellen I won't listen. I'll go to bed.
Catherine (*restraining Ellen*) This is nothing. I was only going to say that heaven did not seem to be my home; and I broke my heart with weeping to come back to earth, and the angels were so angry they flung me out, into the middle of the heath on the top of Wuthering Heights; where I woke, sobbing for joy. There! Now if you think about it *that* will explain my secret. Do you understand, Nelly? I've no more business to marry Edgar Linton than I had to be in heaven; and if Hindley had not brought Heathcliff so low I shouldn't have thought of it. It would degrade me to marry Heathcliff *now*.

At this Heathcliff creeps away unseen by them

Ellen senses his presence and looks up sharply but she is unsure of herself and says nothing

Catherine continues

And that's why he shall *never* know. He shall never know how I love him—and that *not* because he's handsome, Nelly, but because he's more myself than I am. Whatever our souls are made of, his and mine are the same, and Linton's is as different as a moonbeam from lightning, or frost from fire.

Ellen Hush!

Catherine What is the matter, Nelly?

Ellen Hush! Joseph is back and Heathcliff may be with him. I am not sure Heathcliff was not at the back door this moment.

Catherine Oh, he couldn't overhear from there. I will have supper with you and Joseph and Heathcliff. Ask me to sit with you.

Ellen Yes, miss, if you have a mind—

Catherine And watch Heathcliff as I talk to him—I want to be sure that he has no notion of these things.

Ellen Very well.

Catherine He has not, has he? He does not know what being in love is?

Ellen I see no reason he shouldn't know as well as you.

Catherine What do you mean?

Ellen And if *you* are to be his choice he will be the most unfortunate creature that ever was born!

Catherine Nelly!

Ellen As soon as you become Mrs Linton he loses friend, love and all. Have you considered how *you* will bear the separation? And how Heathcliff will bear to be quite deserted in the world? Because, Miss Catherine—

Catherine Heathcliff and I separated? Not as long as I live. Who is to separate us, pray? Oh, that's not what I intend—that's not what I mean. Every Linton on the face of the earth might vanish before I consent to forsake Heathcliff.

Ellen You are talking nonsense, miss.

Catherine He'll be as much to me as he has always been. Edgar must learn to tolerate him at least. He will when he learns my true feelings towards him. I see you think me a selfish wretch, Nelly, don't you understand that if Heathcliff and I married we should be beggars?

Ellen You cannot be serious.

Catherine Whereas if I marry Linton I can aid Heathcliff to rise, and escape from Hindley's power.

Ellen With your husband's money, Miss?

Catherine Edgar is generous, I am sure he is.

Ellen This is the worst reason you have given yet for marrying.

Catherine It is not the worst, it's the best!

Ellen There is ...

Catherine I told you I couldn't fully explain. I don't know how to express it—surely you have some notion that you have an existence beyond you. What would be the use of my creation if I were entirely contained here in this life? Nelly! My great miseries in this world have been Heathcliff's miseries. I have watched and felt each one from the beginning. My great thought in living is Heathcliff. If all else perished, and *he* remained, I should continue to be. If all else remained and he were gone, the universe would turn to a mighty stranger. My love for Linton is like the foliage in the woods. Time will change it, as winter changes the trees. My love for Heathcliff is as the everlasting rocks beneath—rarely seen to give delight, but eternally necessary. Nelly! I *am* Heathcliff—he's always, always in my mind—not as a pleasure, any more than I am always a pleasure to myself—but as my own being!

A mighty thunderclap

Joseph enters

Joseph What's that nowt Heathcliff up to? T'orses must be stabled afore this storm. What does 'e think 'e's about?
Ellen I'll call him. He'll be in the barn I reckon.

Ellen runs off to call Heathcliff

Thunder

Joseph In't barn? I seed him! Fleein' as though th' clappers of 'ell were after 'im across the moor'.
Catherine When was that Joseph? How long ago?
Joseph No more nor a few minutes. As I came to t' cross for Gimmerton—but 'e were none 'eading for Gimmerton. 'E were off up t'bank t' moor.
Catherine Is he in the barn, Nelly?
Joseph In't barn! 'Aven't I just told ye—

Ellen enters

Ellen He is somewhere out of hearing. I shouted at the top of the fold as loud as I could.
Joseph I'd be none surprised if Owld Nick 'asn't got 'im at last!
Catherine (*in a tone Joseph obeys*) Joseph, find him! He must be out there—find him!
Joseph It's nobbut a waste of o'time, I tell ye . . . storm's nearly on us if them 'orses baint stabled . . .

Joseph exits, continuing to grumble

Thunder

Catherine I must speak to him. *I must.* Where is he? Where can he be?
Ellen The gate was open. It's my belief he heard a good part of what you said just now . . .
Catherine Traitor! You knew . . .
Ellen I didn't know and I don't know! I told you at the time.
Catherine How long was he there? When did he go?
Ellen When you said Hindley had brought him so low, it would degrade—
Catherine Oh no! I must find him! (*She goes to run out*)
Ellen Don't be ridiculous! It won't be the first time Heathcliff's taken himself off for the night and more—
Catherine Oh, don't be so stupid, *stupid*—don't you understand? I *must* find him!

She tries to run out, but Ellen drags her back

Thunder

Ellen You will not! What—in this storm!

She forcibly drags Catherine back into the room

Catherine (*breaking down*) Oh, Nelly. What did I say? I've forgotten. Tell me what I said that could grieve him?
Ellen What a noise for nothing! Why—he is as like as not sulking in the hayloft! You just wait, I'll ferret Master Heathcliff out!

Thunder

Ellen is about to go

  Joseph runs in

Joseph Yon lad gets worse and worse! He's left t' gate at full swing and miss's pony 'as trodden down two riggs o' corn!

Catherine runs to him

Catherine Have you found him yet, you ass?
Joseph Maister'll play t' devil in t' morn!
Catherine Have you looked for him, as I ordered? Have you?
Joseph I'll look no further. It's as black as a chimbley an't 'rain's coming across t' moor.
Catherine Then I will! (*She runs to the door*)

Ellen tries to stop her

Ellen No!
Catherine Heathcliff! Let me go! Heathcliff!
Joseph Aye! Heathcliff's noon t'chap to coom at *my* whistle. 'Appen e'll be less hard of hearing wi *ye*!
Catherine Heathcliff!

  Catherine escapes and runs out

A massive crash of thunder, and heavy rain. A great wind rises

Joseph falls to his knees

Joseph
                    O Lord, hear my cry on this Day of Judgement!
                    Remember the Patriarchs, Noah and Lot.
                    And as in former times spare Thou the righteous!

Ellen runs to the stairs

Ellen Mr Earnshaw!
Joseph But if it be Thy will to find out the Sinner. To cleanse the earth of the wicked and smite the ungodly—
Ellen Mr Earnshaw! Mr Earnshaw
Joseph   Seek Thou them out!
                    Strike 'em with thy bolt!
Hindley (*off: shouting over the storm*) Go to bloody hell!
Joseph   Strike 'em!
                    Strike down the wicked!
                    But not till they be out o't' road o' thy servants!
                    Strike 'em!

The loudest thunder-crash. Joseph covers his head and ears. A crash of brickwork falling

Lockwood is watching in the shadows

Ellen (*to Lockwood in narration*) It's the great oak at the corner of the house—it's knocked down the chimney stack.

Catherine enters slowly, drenched

Ellen runs to her

The storm begins to abate

Miss Cathy! Are you bent on catching your death? Come along to bed. He'll have gone to Gimmerton.

Joseph Nay, nay. He were not for Gimmerton. Ah'd never wonder but what 'e were at the bottom of a bog. This visitation weren't for nowt! And I'd 'av you look out, miss—it's thy turn next! Thank 'eaven for all! All works together for t' good o' them that is chozzen an' piked out from th' rubbidge.

Hindley enters

Hindley (*to Catherine*) What ails you, Cathy! You look as dismal and drowned as a whelp.

Catherine I've been wet and I'm cold, that's all. Leave me alone.

Ellen Oh, she's naughty, sir. She's been out in the storm.

Hindley Out in the storm? Why—

Ellen I don't know why—

Catherine (*shivering*) Nelly, Nelly, I'm starving with cold ...

Hindley She's ill.

Ellen And who can wonder?

Hindley Damn it to hell. I don't want any more sickness here! What took you out in the rain?

Joseph (*assuming his full Old Testament air*) Runnin' after t' lads as usual. Never a day y'r off, maister, but yon lad o' Linton's is sneakin' hither. Miss Ellen watches for ye, oh aye, in t'kitchen! As you're out one door, he's in at t'other. (*Glaring at Catherine*) And when she's done wi' t' gentry she's out among t' fields wi' that flaysome devil of a gypsy, Heathcliff! Aw seed yah! Aw seed yah!

Ellen Joseph hold your tongue!

Joseph Ye think I'm blind, but I noan! *You* (*to Nelly*)—you good-for-nowt slatternly witch, I see *thy* game—wickedly playin' t' middle against t' ends! 'Elpin' 'em all on to damnation.

Catherine Stop him, Nelly!

Joseph If I were thee maister, I'd slam t' boards in their wicked faces, gentle and simple like!

Hindley Cathy. Tell me the truth, damn you; were you out with Heathcliff tonight?

Ellen No, she wasn't.

Hindley Speak for yourself! Were you with him tonight?

Catherine (*sobbing*) I never saw Heathcliff tonight.

Hindley Well, we'll sort it for the future. I'll send him packing in the morning.

Catherine No!

Ellen Nay, master ...

Hindley Be quiet and remember your place. Bag and baggage he goes.
Catherine Turn him out, and I shall go with him!
Hindley You'll learn to watch your step, miss! With Heathcliff gone I'll have all the more humour for you—
Catherine Maybe you won't get the chance you've wanted for years—Heathcliff has gone already—gone for ever!

She breaks down completely, and collapses

Hindley God damn you! Be silent! (*To Ellen*) Get her to her room and out of my sight or she'll not weep for nothing!

Joseph and Ellen carry Catherine upstairs, sobbing and struggling

Hindley exits

Lockwood Was she very ill?
Ellen It was the beginning of her first fever. The doctor bled her and ordered us to guard her in her delirium, to see she did not throw herself downstairs or out of the window. From now on she must not be crossed: she must have her own way. (*She comes down and tidies the room*) She lay for months dangerously ill. Old Mrs Linton visited us regularly, and put us to rights, for which kindness she and her husband were rewarded when they both took the fever, and died within two days of each other.
Lockwood And Heathcliff?
Ellen Went into the thunderstorm and was seen and heard of no more.
Lockwood But your mistress recovered?
Ellen For us who live close to the earth the progress of the seasons is the best medicine. Winter passes from the Heights slowly but by April we have the days of great clear skies, fresh winds and the heath is lit by the flame of gorse. Below the valley is filled with spring—and in such days—

The Lights come to full. Ellen moves to the fireplace

Edgar leads Catherine down the stairs. They are laughing

Hindley enters with Edgar

Edgar You know my estate and how well I am provided. I am sad to think my parents are not alive to give us their blessing, this I feel greatly. However . . . I must tell you that by the terms of my father's will, in the absence of a male heir, my sister Isabella will inherit the bulk of the fortune; also, if Isabella marry and produce male issue, and I don't—the estate will likewise go to him—
Hindley So if you do not produce a son or if you die before Catherine—she will be a penniless widow?
Edgar No. She will be well provided for—but the Grange and the bulk of the fortune passes to the *male heir*, mine or Isabella's.
Hindley So it is for Catherine to produce a boy?
Edgar (*smiling*) To inherit in full—yes.
Hindley Then if she fails in her duty, let it be her own funeral.
Catherine Hindley, I must have Nelly with me at the Grange!
Ellen No! I cannot leave Wuthering Heights!

Catherine I won't be crossed. Tell her she must come.

Ellen Miss Catherine—Mr Hindley and you, too sir. With respect it seems to me that little *Hareton* must be considered before all. He can't be left with the men—without the nurse who has been like his mother . . .

Hindley (*bitterly*) Like his mother but not his mother!

Edgar I will more than double your wages, Mrs Dean! There is no cost too high or any I'll begrudge to make my wife as happy as she can possibly be!

Catherine There you are Nelly—what could be more generous?

Ellen No! I cannot leave Hareton!

Hindley Pack your traps and move to the Grange as soon as you are required. Now there is no mistress here I want no women in the house.

Ellen No!

Hindley As for Hareton, the curate can take him in hand by and by.

Ellen But, sir—

Hindley (*stopping further argument*) You've no choice. Do as you're told.

Ellen (*in tears*) Very well. I must do as I am told. But you do not deceive me, sir! I know you only rid yourself of decent people about the place so that you may go to the devil all the faster.

Hindley Enough, woman! (*To Edgar*) You are welcome to them both!

Hindley exits

Catherine crosses to Edgar, and they stand wrapped in each other's arms

The Lights trap down

Ellen moves down to Lockwood

Ellen So, sir, that is when I came to Thrushcross Grange. Eighteen years ago. Miss Catherine, Mrs Linton I must call her now, took well to her new surroundings and seemed fond, even over-fond, of her husband and showed plenty of affection for Isabella.

Edgar and Catherine move slowly away

I really believe they were in possession of a deep and growing happiness.

Lockwood What of little Hareton? What of him?

Ellen looks back on Wuthering Heights as the lights fade on it

Ellen I kissed him goodbye. Since then he has been a stranger. It is very queer to think of it, sir, but I have no doubt he has forgotten all about Ellen Dean and that he was ever more than all the world to her, and she to him.

CURTAIN

ACT II

Thrushcross Grange

Catherine, Ellen and Isabella are sitting knitting or sewing baby garments which they show to each other at what is evidently the end of a session devoted to such work

There is a large window enclosure and a couch

Ellen (*to Lockwood*) And on a mellow evening in September—it ended.
Catherine There now! I think, Isabella, we have almost enough to clothe your first three nephews, providing Edgar and I are not blessed with twins!

Lockwood exits

Ellen (*as she collects the sewing gear and garments*)
         Pink is for a little girl
         Blue for a boy
         Cradle trimmings, Christening robe:
         White for parents joy ...
Catherine And whichever it is, it will be welcome, although I hope one of the first three will be a boy to please Edgar!
Isabella (*a little coolly*) Yes, an heir will be splendid.
Catherine Even though it disinherits you, I am afraid I must wish it, Isabella.
Isabella The most natural thing in the world, my dear, and be sure I wish it too.
Ellen Such things are the will of heaven.
Catherine Bless your golden little heart, Isabella, I don't question your generosity; I know you have Edgar's happiness very much in mind.
Isabella Yours too, Catherine dear. I think, though, the sewing has given me just a touch of headache; you will excuse me if I retire?
Catherine Away with you and lie down, you shouldn't let the work tire you.
Ellen I had better think about tea; the master will be ready for his, I am sure.
Isabella (*as she goes*) I will come back for tea, and lie down afterwards.

Isabella exits

Catherine And I will go and entice Edgar from his books.

Ellen exits

Edgar comes in

Edgar Am I permitted to inspect the results of the afternoon's work?
Catherine Later, Edgar. Nelly has put it away. I was just coming to fetch you.
Edgar Then let us sit in the window; and wait for her. These late summer evenings are delightful—the light is just fading—we shall soon have autumn upon us.
Catherine You can still see beyond the orchard and the park.

Edgar The whole valley is a sea of silvery mist.
Catherine And rising proudly above it—Wuthering Heights.
Edgar How are you feeling today, my love?
Catherine I am very well indeed, and quite content.

Ellen enters

They pay no attention to her and she watches them for a moment sitting quietly in the last of the afternoon sun. It is a very peaceful picture

Edgar (*noticing her*) What is it, Nelly?
Ellen (*uneasy*) I wondered—should I bring the tea up here, sir.
Catherine Of course, Nelly.

Ellen turns to go, hesitates

Edgar Was there something else?
Ellen Oh and, a person from Gimmerton wishes to see you, ma'am.
Catherine (*without moving*) What does he want?
Ellen I didn't question him.
Catherine Well, close the curtains when the light goes, and bring the tea, Nelly. (*She rises, kisses Edgar lightly and goes to the door*) I'll be back again directly.

Catherine exits

The sun sets and it becomes progressively darker outside. In the room the firelight begins to take effect

There is a slight pause and then Edgar speaks

Edgar Who is it, Nelly?
Ellen (*busying herself about the room*) Someone the mistress doesn't expect! Oh, dear I wonder—oh! (*She clatters the fire-irons in annoyance*)
Edgar What's the matter?
Ellen It's that Heathcliff. You recollect him, sir? Heathcliff who used to live at Wuthering Heights.
Edgar What, Nelly! You mean the gypsy—the ploughboy?
Ellen Hush—please, sir . . .
Edgar I don't understand. Is this a matter of consequence?
Ellen You must not call him by those names sir. The mistress would be sadly hurt.
Edgar Really? They were very close as children—I know that of course—but they are not children now—so—I really don't understand; you seem quite agitated.
Ellen He came upon me so suddenly—it was such a surprise. I didn't think—I see now, sir, I am to blame—I shouldn't have heeded him when he bade me give that message: "Just say 'a person from Gimmerton to see you.' " I should have told *you* sir.
Edgar If my wife had wanted to speak to him she would have gone in any case—there's no harm done.
Ellen They were more like brother and sister, and later on—she was heartbroken when he ran off; oh dear, I shouldn't have been so foolish and overawed by the man!
Edgar (*a little irritably*) Nelly, this is nothing; we'll dispose of it in a minute.

Ellen As you say, sir, and I hope you are right. And, as you say, sir, they are not
children now—I hope you will remember those words, sir—(*quickly before he can
silence her*)—and all I know is, sir, his return will make a jubileee for her!

Edgar goes to the window and, after watching for a moment, opens it

Edgar Don't stand out there, my love. Bring the person in, if it be anyone particular.
(*He closes the window before there can be a reply and comes into the room with a
slightly troubled expression*) You had better bring the tea, Nelly.

*Before Ellen can move, the door flies open and Catherine bursts in, wild with
excitement. She rushes to Edgar and flings her arms around his neck*

Catherine Oh, Edgar, Edgar! Oh Edgar, darling! Heathcliff's come back—he is!
Edgar (*crossly*) Well, well, don't strangle me for that.
Catherine But he's back! Standing outside this very minute!
Edgar He never struck me as such a marvellous treasure. There is no need to be
frantic.

Ellen exits

Catherine I know you didn't like him.
Edgar I wouldn't say that. I hardly noticed him.
Catherine Yet, for my sake, you must be friends now. You will?
Edgar Catherine, we are not children any longer, none of us. You are no longer—
Catherine Shall I tell him to come in?
Edgar Here? Into the parlour?
Catherine Where else?
Edgar (*snappishly*) In the kitchen I should think.

*She stands away from him, regarding him with a droll expression, half anger, half
amusement*

Catherine No. I don't feel the kitchen.

Ellen enters with tea

Ah, Nelly! Set the tea at two separate tables! One for your master and Isabella,
being gentry, *there*. The other, for Heathcliff and myself, being of the lower orders,
here. (*Moving across the room away from the door, to Edgar*) Will that please you,
dear?
Edgar Catherine, there is absolutely no need—
Catherine Or must I have a fire lighted elsewhere?
Edgar Catherine there is absolutely no need—
Catherine If so, give orders. (*She begins to move to the door*) I'll run down and secure
my guest.

Edgar intercepts her

Edgar (*To Ellen*) Nelly! *You* bid him step up.

Ellen goes

And you, Catherine, try to be glad without being absurd.

She looks at him doubtfully then slowly goes to the window

Catherine I wonder if I am about to see an unsuspected side of your nature?
Edgar The whole household need not witness the sight of you welcoming a runaway
    servant as a brother.
Catherine (*working up to an outburst*) Oh dear, what a little ass you can be!
Edgar Once and for all, before there is any development—
Ellen Mr Heathcliff.

Heathcliff, immaculately dressed, is shown in by Ellen

*Catherine's ill-humour appears to vanish instantly in a smile. She goes to Heathcliff,
takes both his hands in hers and, crossing to Edgar, takes one hand of his and crushes it
into Heathcliff's. Edgar, amazed at the change in Heathcliff, is at a loss. Heathcliff lets
go the hand and coolly stands waiting for Edgar to speak*

Edgar Sit down, sir. Mrs Linton, recalling old times, would have me give you a
    cordial reception and of course I am gratified when anything occurs to please her.
Heathcliff I also. If it be anything in which I have part.
Edgar (*stiffly*) Then you are welcome, sir.
Heathcliff Good. Then I will stay a while with pleasure. (*He goes to sit*)

*Catherine almost dances about; she catches hold of Heathcliff's hands again and sits him
beside her on a sofa. She seems oblivious of her husband's presence*

Catherine I shall think this a dream tomorrow! I shall not be able to believe I have
    seen and touched and spoken to you once more. Yet you don't deserve this
    welcome—three years of silence—and you never thought of me.
Heathcliff A little more than you thought of me! I came back with a plan. Then I
    heard you were married. So I must modify the plan. I thought about this very hard,
    just now, while I waited below in the yard.

The power of his personality holds them in silence while he looks from one to the other

    Your welcome has put these things from my mind!
Catherine Oh Heathcliff!
Heathcliff You'll not drive me off again. I have fought through a bitter life since last I
    heard your voice and you must forgive me, because I struggled only for you.
Edgar Catherine, unless we are to have cold tea—
Catherine Yes, now, let us have tea. Tea, Heathcliff?
Edgar (*striving to preserve an ordinary tone and a measure of politeness*) Mr Heathcliff
    will have a long walk wherever he may lodge tonight—and I'm thirsty!
Catherine You haven't rung for Isabella.

He does so

*Catherine pours out tea. She never touches hers. Edgar hardly touches his; only
Heathcliff, completely at ease, finishes his*

Ellen comes in

Ellen Miss Isabella is not feeling well, sir and asks to be excused.
Edgar Tell her I will come to her presently.
Catherine Does she know Mr Heathcliff is here?
Ellen No ma'am. Unless she saw him approach through the park.
Edgar You must tell her the great news, Nelly.

Ellen goes out

Are you going to tell us your adventures, sir?

Heathcliff No.

Edgar I am sorry I cannot offer you . . .

Heathcliff (*without looking at him*) I expect nothing from you, sir, I shall stay at Wuthering Heights.

Catherine The Heights?

Heathcliff Hindley invited me when I called this morning.

Catherine Hindley!

Heathcliff Invited me. And indeed, now you know of my—availability—I must go. (*He rises*) It has been a short stay, but a pleasant one.

Catherine Going so soon? This is ridiculous. Edgar, make him stay!

Heathcliff Well, Mr Linton, are you inclined to make me stay?

Catherine You mustn't tease Edgar.

Edgar I am inclined to respect my guest's wishes and speed him on his way.

Heathcliff I thank you, sir. I shall come again—always being careful of course not to outwear my welcome!

Without any further formality Heathcliff goes

Catherine is about to follow him but Edgar prevents her

Edgar Ellen will see him out.

Catherine runs to the window and then comes back to Edgar

Catherine Yes—he'll have a fine old talk to Nelly! She will know far more of his past doings and his future intentions than us! Oh, Edgar, you can be tiresome. Why didn't you encourage him to stay and tell us about himself?

Edgar You must give me credit for making the attempt.

Catherine You are sulking because I'm glad of something that does not interest you.

Edgar That is most unkind. You cannot expect me to respond to your Heathcliff in any other way. I have always had an aversion to him.

Catherine Of course, and why? Because he was always dirty and rough—can't you understand, he was purposely reduced to that state by Hindley? That was not his real nature. And look at him now! Isn't he quite the gentleman? Isn't he worth anyone's regard?

Edgar I cannot continue with this—you are cruel and selfish.

Catherine And you are silly and pettish.

Edgar I am going to my study and I would appreciate not being disturbed for the remainder of the evening.

Catherine Oh, go to your study! Go and snivel and think yourself badly done to! There are times when I could shake you!

Edgar goes without replying

Catherine goes to the window, which she opens, and calls

Goodbye, Heathcliff, come again soon!

After a moment Ellen comes in

Nelly. I want to know all that has passed between you and Heathcliff. Edgar has gone to his study in a pet.

Ellen Look, ma'am—you must be careful what you are about—

Catherine Why? I have no need to be careful when I am open and frank and have nothing to hide. No. Isabella and Edgar are both alike and always have been—spoilt children. I humour them, but I think they would improve just the same with a good smart slap.

Ellen You are mistaken, Mrs Linton; they humour *you*! And if you fall out over something of equal consequence to you both, you may well find those you think weak are as obstinate as you!

Catherine (*gaily*) Then we shall fight to the death, shan't we Nelly? No—I have such faith in Edgar's love that I think I might torture him to death and he would let me do it.

Ellen You should value him more for his affection.

Catherine I do. But he must get used to Heathcliff. Instead of whining and weeping when I said Heathcliff was worthy of regard—he should have said it for me! He should have been delighted to see the great change in my friend.

Ellen You cannot expect the master to be *delighted*.

Catherine I tell you he is going to become accustomed to him, so he may as well like him!

Ellen And am *I* bidden to like him? I was often sorry for Heathcliff in the old days; I think Hindley used him badly, I don't think I ever *liked* him. I think . . .

Catherine What you think doesn't matter, you're not important, be quiet! Oh, I'm sorry, Nelly, but oh! . . . considering how Heathcliff has reason to object to *him*—I don't care what you say—I think Heathcliff behaved splendidly.

Ellen He looked splendid, yes . . . who would ever have thought the time would come when I would find myself compelled to say "Mister" Heathcliff!

Catherine I can't understand his going to Wuthering Heights. Is he offering the hand of friendship to his enemies all round?

Ellen He went to Wuthering Heights to find *me*, to ask of news of *you*—he thought that I still lived there.

Catherine And Hindley invited him to stay—doubtless to gamble. Hindley would only have him around at a price—Heathcliff seems to be rich. It is strange though.

Ellen Very strange. Have you no fear of the consequences, Mrs Linton?

Catherine None for Heathcliff! He can take care of himself!

Ellen You must know the tales that are going around about Hindley.

Catherine Nelly, I never did care and I don't care now what becomes of Hindley! The event of this evening has reconciled me to God and humanity! Heathcliff is back!

Ellen And you're not afraid—

Catherine Don't spoil my happiness.

Ellen You are in a queer mood.

Catherine I'm happy! Very well, Mrs Dean—I'm rebuked—but Nelly, dear Nelly—

Ellen Now don't say anything I shall be sorry to hear—such things are not my concern—and I have a duty to Mr Edgar—

Catherine I'll go and make my peace with Edgar instantly. And what is more, I shall ask him to let me visit Heathcliff at Wuthering Heights.

Ellen Miss Catherine!

Catherine Never fear—Isabella shall chaperone me. Don't worry, Nelly—I'm an angel!

Catherine dances off: When she is gone Ellen speaks to Lockwood in the shadows

Ellen Yes, madam, and there is a bit of the other thing in you—and always was. A wild wicked slip she was! Ready at a whim to lead the whole house a dance—but always with the gift of prevailing with those she'd injured. Mr Edgar emerged from his gloom, allowed her and Isabella to visit, and she rewarded him with such a time of sweetness and affection, as made the house a paradise. He was not to know that his next tribulation was to come very close at hand, and darken the remainder of his life:

Ellen exits with Lockwood

Sunlight illuminates Isabella as she walks to the window. She is singing a sweet, simple song

Catherine enters by the door and watches her, listening

Catherine How pleasant to hear you happy—what has happened to bring this change about? For the last month you have been drifting about the house and park like a lost soul. I can't tell you how Edgar has been worried. Is it the sunny day that has raised your spirits?

Isabella You want me to tell you the reason? Of course you do. And you are going to be pleased.

Catherine It is such a happy relief.

Isabella Heathcliff is coming.

Catherine Where? (*moving to her side at the window*) Can you see him outside?

Isabella No, not yet. He is coming though—and this time particularly to see me.

Catherine I hope I am not hearing properly.

Isabella He said I might expect him today. All I want is to be . . .

Catherine Well?

Isabella With him—and I won't always be sent off!

Catherine Who sends you off?

Isabella *You.* You always find an excuse to send me away.

Catherine Don't dare tell me such stories—

Isabella And I know why, Cathy—I am not quite as childish as you think; you don't want anyone to be loved except yourself.

Catherine You need a slap, miss—

Isabella You are a dog in the manger—

Catherine And you are an impertinent little monkey! I'll not believe this idiocy! It is impossible that you can covet the admiration of Heathcliff—that you consider him an agreeable person! I hope I have misunderstood you, Isabella!

Isabella No you have not. I love him.

Catherine Quiet! For God's sake.

Isabella I love him more than you love Edgar. And he might love me if you would let him!

Catherine I wouldn't be you for a kingdom then!

Isabella You would give your sight and half your life to be me—don't pretend!

Catherine Listen to me—there are, things about life and people that you can't possibly understand yet—you have not had the chance—or the time—

Isabella Did you gather all your wisdom there amongst the rustics?

Catherine Yes. More than you ever did in your parlour.

Isabella Do you think of Edgar like this?

Catherine Heathcliff is an unreclaimed creature; fierce, pitiless, wolfish. He'll crush you like a sparrow's egg. Let him alone or God help you! Heathcliff could never love a Linton. There—that's my picture of him and I am his friend.

Isabella Yes Cathy, I can hear—you sound very much like Heathcliff's friend!

Catherine You won't believe me? You think I speak from selfish wickedness?

Isabella I know you do. And I shudder at you!

Catherine Will you listen to me—

Isabella I'll listen no more. You are worse than twenty enemies—it is you who are the poisonous friend—

Catherine (*her temper suddenly going*) Try for yourself—if that be your spirit! Try for yourself!

Ellen enters

Ellen Mr Heathcliff, ma'am. (*She goes to attend the fire*)

Isabella, with downcast eyes, unable to escape, turns away, sits, opens a book, pretends to read

Heathcliff enters

Catherine becomes instantly excessively gay

Catherine Come in, come in Heathcliff! Here are two people sadly in need of a third to thaw the ice between them!

Heathcliff (*indifferently*) Indeed, what's amiss?

Catherine (*crossing behind where Isabella sits and throwing her arms about her*) Heathcliff, I am proud to show you at last someone who dotes on you more than I do! My poor little sister-in-law is breaking her heart at the mere contemplation of your physical and moral beauty!

Heathcliff Is she indeed?

Catherine It lies in your power to become Edgar's brother! No, no, Isabella, you shan't run off. *You* may, Nelly, thank you.

Ellen exits

We were quarrelling like cats about you, Heathcliff—and I was beaten! I was informed that if I had but the manners to stand aside, my rival here would shoot a shaft into your soul to fix you for ever and send me to eternal oblivion!

Isabella Catherine, I would thank you to keep to the truth and not slander me. Mr Heathcliff, be kind enough to bid this friend of yours release me. What amuses her is painful to me beyond expression.

Heathcliff looks at them coldly

Isabella twists in Catherine's hold and cries in supplication

Catherine!

Catherine No, you shan't go! I'll not be called a dog in the manger again. You *shall* stay. Now then, Heathcliff, aren't you pleased at my news? Can't you see how she is straining at the leash to throw herself into your arms?

Heathcliff I think you belie her—she is rather straining to be out of my reach—there will be tears in a moment.

Isabella suddenly uses her nails on Catherine, frees herself, rushes to the door and exits

Catherine There's a tigress! Begone for God's sake and hide your vixen face! See those talons, Heathcliff. You must beware your eyes.

Heathcliff I'd wrench them off her finger if they menaced me.

Catherine Could you honestly resist those baby-blue eyes?

Heathcliff I'd soon turn them black—they remind me damnably of Linton's. Ha! I remember her looking me over in my stable-boy's rig when she visited the Heights as a child. I itched to toss her in the horse muck, then!

Catherine I keep being told you are a gentleman—pray don't use such coarse expressions.

Heathcliff I am still the Heathcliff you always knew—I have not altered, except outwardly—remember that. Nor have you.

Catherine Except that I have become a married woman!

Heathcliff Don't remind me.

She goes silently to the window. There is a pause

That girl, Isabella—she is her brother's heir isn't she?

Catherine I should be sorry to think so. My son shall remove her title, please heaven!

Heathcliff And if it is a daughter—

Catherine It'll be a son, Heathcliff.

Ellen enters

Ellen The master is coming, ma'am.

Heathcliff I have no mind to hold polite conversation with Linton. Will you ride with me tomorrow?

Catherine Ride, in my condition?

Heathcliff Then walk.

Catherine Why can you not stay now?

Edgar comes in

Edgar Well sir, how are things at the Heights?

Heathcliff By now the Heights is largely mortgaged to me—we play at cards. You should be gratified that I effect my purpose in so civilized a way. Were he not Catherine's brother, his corpse might long ago—

Catherine Heathcliff! It is time you removed yourself from the Heights. Why in heaven's name you are there I can't think.

Heathcliff So that I may be near you! Your servant, sir.

Heathcliff bows to them and goes quietly through the door

Edgar I wonder sometimes if that man is human. I don't disguise from you, Catherine, that his visits are becoming a nightmare to me. With your confinement there must be a break and afterwards if they persist I shall consider taking you away.

Catherine You won't take me anywhere I don't want to go.

"Edgar's hand went to his eyes as if to hide a sudden rush of tears and without another word he left the room"

Ellen, who has been occupied in a distant corner of the room, comes to Catherine in indignation

Ellen It is a sin to see such a gentle, kind master used so ...

Catherine Look to your business woman, and stop this eavesdropping.

Ellen Look! (*She points through the window*) Judas!

Catherine Who?

Ellen (*pointing*) Your worthless friend.

Catherine follows Ellen's accusing finger

See! He has caught a glimpse of us and he is coming back. Kissing Miss Isabella before your very eyes!

Heathcliff comes in

You're a villain! I curse the day you ever came back!

Catherine Hold your tongue! To hear you, people might think *you* were the mistress here! Heathcliff—what are you about raising this stir?

Heathcliff goes to Catherine

No ...

Heathcliff Cathy!

Catherine I know you too well to heed a word of explanation. It would be a lie. Leave Isabella alone, do you hear! Absolutely alone from this instant unless you are tired of being received here and wish Linton to draw the bolts against you!

Heathcliff Let him try! Every day I grow madder to send him to heaven!

Catherine Did that slut come across you on purpose?

Heathcliff What is it to you? I have a right to kiss her, if she chooses and you have no right to object. I'm not *your* husband ...

Catherine No, no, I know ...

Heathcliff (*overlapping her words*) ... you needn't be jealous of me!

Catherine I'm not jealous of you—Heathcliff, I'm jealous *for* you—clear your face— you shan't scowl at me! You know I'll do anything to keep you by. If you like Isabella, you shall marry her. But do you want to? Do you? There, you won't answer—I *know* you don't!

Ellen Mr Linton would never consent—

Catherine Mr Linton will do as I say—(*to Ellen*)and you—out!

Ellen goes

Heathcliff He can spare himself the trouble. But *you*, Catherine—I'll be silent no longer. You've brought me to hell! You've treated me infernally—infernally! Do you hear? Don't flatter yourself that I can be consoled by a few sweet words—or that I will suffer unrevenged! Meanwhile, thank you for little Miss Isabella's secret—I swear I'll make the most of it.

Catherine What do you mean—I've treated you infernally? You'll take revenge? How?

Heathcliff I seek no revenge on *you*. That's not the plan. You are welcome to torture me to death for your own amusement—just allow me to do the same. And don't patronize me! If I imagined you really wished me to marry Isabella, I'd cut my throat!

Catherine Oh—the evil is that I'm *not* jealous, is that it? You scorn my offer of a wife—?

Heathcliff *Your* offer? Do you think I need *you*? See what I have made of myself—to one end; to possess you and be master of the Heights and the Grange; I'd torture a whole generation to get my way—to bring my enemies grovelling to the pig trough where they belong *and I will do it*!

Catherine You're mad! Your bliss lies, like the devil's, in fetching down misery—no, you'll hear me!—You prove it. Edgar is restored from the ill-humour your return caused—by me. I begin to be secure and tranquil and you are determined to wreck the only peaceful solution there can be. Very well. Quarrel with Edgar. Deceive his sister—you'll revenge yourself on me!

Edgar enters

Edgar (*to Heathcliff*) This is insufferable. (*To Catherine*) It is disgraceful that you should want to own this man as a friend—you'll have no further dealings with him. I have humoured you enough!

Catherine Have you been listening at the door, Edgar?

Heathcliff gives a sneering laugh

Edgar I have so far been forbearing with you, sir. But your presence is a moral poison. To prevent further consequences, I shall deny you hereafter admission into this house and give notice now that I require your instant departure. Three minutes delay will render it involuntary and ignominious.

Heathcliff (*looking him over with an eye full of derision*) Cathy, this lamb of yours threatens like a bull! It is in danger of splitting its skull against my knuckles. By God, Linton, I am mortally sorry you are not worth knocking down!

Edgar looks quickly to the door. Catherine runs to it and turns the key in the lock. She looks at Edgar with contempt

Catherine I knew it! Your men are outside! But they shan't get in! (*She holds up the key*)

Edgar Catherine, give me that key.

Catherine Fair means! If you have not the courage to assert yourself, apologize! Apologize to Heathcliff *now* or take the thrashing you deserve!

Edgar (*clearly shaken*) Catherine! Give me that key at once.

Catherine I'll swallow it before you get it!

They struggle. She throws the key out of the window

And now I'll watch this! *I'll* have a little revenge. Oh I am delightfully rewarded for my kindness to you both! After constant indulgence of one's weak nature and the other's bad one, I earn for thanks two samples of blind ingratitude, stupid to

absurdity! Edgar! I was defending you and yours: and I wish Heathcliff may flog
you sick for daring to think an evil thought of me!

Edgar, overcome, sits at the table, his head in his hands

Oh! Look at this! We are lost, lost! (*She goes close to Edgar and almost hisses in his
ear*) Heathcliff would as soon lift a finger at you as the King would march his army
against a colony of mice! Cheer up! You shan't be hurt! Your type is not a lamb, it's
a sucking leveret!

There is a considerable banging and thrusting at the door

Heathcliff strolls to the window and throws a leg over the sill

Heathcliff (*as he goes*) Is he weeping or is he going to faint for fear? I compliment you
on your taste! This is the slavering, shivering thing your preferred to me! I wish you
joy of him!

He jumps out of the window

There is a slight pause then Edgar, still seated, speaks quietly and without anger

Edgar Catherine. I want only to know now whether you intend to continue this
intimacy with ...

Catherine Oh for mercy's sake! (*at the door*) Stop that banging, you clowns, and be
off!

The noise outside stops

Your man's half way across the park.

Edgar Catherine!

Catherine (*to Edgar*) For mercy's sake not now! Your cold blood cannot be worked
into a fever—your veins are full of ice-water, mine are boiling; just be quiet, or go!

Edgar To get rid of me, answer my question. Your violence doesn't alarm me. Will
you give up Heathcliff hereafter or will you give up me?

Catherine I'll wrangle no more!

Edgar Choose. I absolutely require to know which you choose.

Catherine I require to be let alone! I demand it! (*Calling*) Nelly! You have a key, open
this door! Oh God! God! God!

*"She threw herself on the sofa and gave way to a senseless, wicked rage, dashing her
head against the arm and grinding her teeth so that you might fancy she would crush
them to splinters"*

The door is opened by Ellen with a key from her chatelaine

Edgar Nelly, fetch some water quickly!

Ellen There is nothing in the world the matter, sir.

Edgar She has blood on her lips.

Ellen Mr Linton, this is a woman's work—leave me. Send at once for Dr Kenneth
and the midwife—just in case.

Edgar Catherine, my dear, my love ...

Catherine twists away from him

Nelly, look after her well—I'll do as you say.

Edgar exits

Ellen Now ma'am! Enough of this play-acting—your husband's gone and you'll deal with me! Come along now—

Catherine Oh, Nelly, Nelly, I'm distracted! A thousand smiths' hammers beat in my brain—leave me alone. Leave me alone and tell Isabella to shun me. This uproar is due to her—I will run wild!

Ellen You must be still.

Catherine Edgar doesn't love me any more—What possessed him to listen at the door? I'll make him sorry! If I were sure it would destroy him, I'd kill myself now!

Ellen Catherine! Do you wish to lose your baby?

Catherine (*backing away*) You don't like me—how strange—I thought everyone hated one another, but couldn't help loving me! They are all turned enemies! How dreary to meet death surrounded by their cold faces—Isabella terrified and repelled, Edgar standing solemnly by to see it over, then offering thanks to God for restoring peace to his house—No!

Ellen Come along to bed.

Catherine Let none of them near me—I'll take no food nor drink—For I will surely break their hearts by breaking mine—I care not how long it takes—I care not how long . . .

Catherine backs away and exits

The Lights fade

Lockwood enters in the shadows

Ellen (*to Lockwood*) And while, day after day, Catherine wore herself away at Thrushcross Grange, refusing food to the point of starvation, inviting death by exposure to the chill night air as she gazed across the valley—

Lockwood To Wuthering Heights.

Ellen Heathcliff began to put into action his long-meditated plan of revenge.

The Lights come up on Wuthering Heights

Isabella, wrapped in a travelling-cloak enters and stands gazing fearfully around her. She starts as Joseph steps out of the shadows

Isabella Where is Mr Heathcliff?

Joseph Whut?

Isabella Will you stay with me until someone comes?

Joseph Mim, mim, mim—Did ever a Christian body 'ear 'owt like it? 'Ow can ah tell wot y' say?

Isabella I say, I wish you would stay with me until someone comes.

Joseph Nay—not me! Ah gotten summat else t' do.

Joseph exits

After a short suspense a tall, gaunt man enters from above, without neckerchief and otherwise extremely slovenly, his features lost in masses of shaggy hair that hang on his shoulders: It is Hindley

Hindley What's your business here? Who are you?

Isabella My name was Isabella Linton. You've seen me before.

Hindley Was?

Isabella I am Mrs Heathcliff—lately married—he took me away—now he has brought me here, I suppose by your permission.

Hindley Is he come back then?

Isabella Yes, we came back just now and he left me in the kitchen. When I would have looked about me, your little boy played sentinel with a bulldog—

Hindley It's well the hellish villain has kept his word! The son of a gypsy's bitch ...

Isabella I am tired with my journey and I want to go to bed! Where is the maid-servant?

Hindley ranges up and down, ignoring her

Tell me where she is as she won't come to me!

Hindley We have none.

Isabella Where must I sleep then?

Hindley Joseph will show you Heathcliff's chamber.

Isabella goes to move. Hindley seizes her

And watch you draw your bolt—turn your lock—don't forget!

Isabella Very well. But why, Mr Earnshaw?

Hindley Look here! (*He produces from his coat a curiously constructed pistol, with a double-edged spring knife attached to the barrel*) That's a great tempter to a desperate man, is it not? Every night I go up and try his door. If once I find it open, he's done for! Though I have a hundred reasons for keeping him alive—

Isabella Mr Earnshaw—

Hindley Not all the angels in heaven shall save him!

Isabella Mr Earnshaw—give me that—weapon, allow me to put it somewhere safe—

Hindley You think I'm mad and must be humoured? Nothing of the kind! I don't care if you tell him. Put him on his guard—and watch for him. Now you know the terms we are on.

Isabella What has Heathcliff done to you?

Hindley I see his danger does not shock you.

Isabella If he has wronged you so that you hate him so much wouldn't it be wiser to bid him quit the house?

Hindley NO! Should he offer to leave me he's a dead man! Persuade him to attempt it and you're a murderess!

Isabella You must have a dreadful reason to ...

Hindley Am I to lose all—with no chance to win it back? Is Hareton to be a beggar? (*He ranges about the great room speaking to himself rather than Isabella*) Damnation, I will win it back. And I'll have his gold too, and then, I'll have his blood and hell shall have his soul! ... Where is he? Joseph!

Joseph enters

Where is Heathcliff? Show this woman to his room.

Joseph Tha knows, maister, that 'e allus keeps it locked; he's got t' key.

Hindley (*to Isabella*) Then you'll have to stay there.

Hindley goes up the stairs

Isabella You've got a nice house, Joseph! Pleasant inmates! I think all the madness of all the lunatics in the world settled in my head the day I linked my fate with theirs!

Joseph Then get thyself back t' t' Grange.
Isabella (*beginning to weep*) To think my comfortable old home is but four miles away—it might as well be across the ocean.
Joseph Well, as ye mak' y' bed so ye mun lie on't. 'E's 'ere.

Heathcliff comes in

Joseph goes

Isabella Why did you leave me so long? And I can't get into our room, you took the key.

Heathcliff stares at Isabella

It's locked!
Heathcliff *Our* room? It is not, and it never shall be *yours*. Find yourself somewhere; sleep with Hareton.
Isabella Since we married you have not been kind to me, but existence has been tolerable and I truly thought that things would change. Why have you brought me here to this dreadful place? Do you know that man—Hindley Earnshaw, who, if he is not over the edge of madness is close to it—do you know he roams about the place threatening your life?

Hindley comes down the stairs

Heathcliff No gaming tonight? Where are all our playfellows? Don't tell me we've been deserted?
Hindley We are alone tonight.
Heathcliff And strangely sober—it is a pity we are not to play—you might, with a tolerably clear head, get your revenge.
Hindley I don't play unless witnesses are present.
Heathcliff Still, I'm glad to find you sober—I'm glad to know there are times when you are clear enough to—what is the word—"evaluate"?—Yes, evaluate your position. It gives me satisfaction.
Hindley You're a monster.
Heathcliff Whatever I am, Hindley Earnshaw, I am what you made me. It was easy for you, in your position, to bring me to the level of a beast. I took up the occupation late in life; I'll make a good job of it; I'll see you come to the edge of your grave a pauper.
Hindley That is as may be . . .
Heathcliff As it is I'll be satisfied to see you safely under with the knowledge that your son will be a beggar—like I was once—and you can be sure he'll receive the same treatment.
Hindley I was little more than a child when you were brought here—you came with your master, the devil's assistance. Why shouldn't I resent you? For countless generations my fathers have been masters of Wuthering Heights . . .
Heathcliff No more!
Hindley Look here. (*He points to an inscription in stone above the fireplace*) Hareton Earnshaw, fifteen hundred, and in the parish records their names occur way back before that . . .
Heathcliff But no more Hindley, you are the last!

Hindley Heathcliff—don't ride too high too soon—before the proper witnesses I'll either win back my son's inheritance or—understand I speak my sober intention— I'll find you asleep and cut your throat like the cur you are—Wuthering Heights may fall to ruin, but it will never be inherited by a discarded Lascar's bastard.

Heathcliff strikes him with such force that he falls to the ground and lies still

Isabella screams

Joseph comes running in

Heathcliff I could finish you now but it is more convenient to wait.
Joseph What's there to do now? What's up? O Lord, deliver us!
Heathcliff There's this to do. Your master's mad and if he lives another month I'll have him in an asylum.
Isabella He's bleeding.
Heathcliff Down, you toothless dog and nurse him, do you expect me to stoop?
Joseph If ever I saw a seeght like this may the Lord ...
Heathcliff Down! (*He pushes him on his knees into the pool of blood*)

Joseph puts his hands together and begins to pray

Joseph Lord in Thy mercy ...

Isabella laughs hysterically

Heathcliff Oh, you're amused are you, madam? I forgot you! This is work for you— that's the sort of thing you're fit for—down with you, wash up that mess and quit my sight.

Heathcliff makes to go

Isabella and Joseph struggle with Hindley and get him off behind the settle as the Lights fade

The more the worms writhe, the more I yearn to crush out their entrails. I have no pity! I have no pity!

Heathcliff exits

A Light comes up on Thrushcross Grange. Catherine is in a nightdress, wandering, her hair loose and a distant look in her eye. She holds a pillow from which feathers are escaping. She chases a few and then settles to examine them

Ellen follows her

Catherine (*plucking out the feathers*) That's a wild duck—this is a pigeon's—and here's a moor-cock's, and—I should know it among a thousand, it's a lapwing's! Bonny bird: wheeling over our heads in the middle of the moor. It wanted to get to its nest, for the clouds touched the swells, and it felt rain coming. We picked this feather up from the heath—it wasn't shot. I made Heathcliff promise he'd never shoot a lapwing after, and he didn't—Yet here are more! Did he shoot my lapwings, Nelly? Did he?

Ellen takes the pillow from her

Ellen Here's a mess, now! And no more of that talk. You're wandering. Lie down, now. Shut your eyes.

Ellen helps Catherine to the couch

Catherine Oh, if I were but in my own bed at Wuthering Heights! Scratching my name on the sill. And that wind sounding in the firs by the lattice. Let me feel it, Nelly—it comes straight down the moor—let me have one breath!

Ellen opens the window for a moment. The wind blasts in. Catherine breathes it in, then lies still. She seems to sleep

Ellen closes the window and continues her narrative

Ellen There! Exhaustion had entirely subdued her spirit. Our fiery Catherine subdued at last, no more than an ailing child. I was uneasy; not on her account. She was no different from yesterday or the day before. No. I had been downstairs just now; the dogs were standing guard, hairs raised staring fixedly at the door—waiting for somebody—

Catherine cries out and sits up

What is it now? Are we to have no rest tonight?

Catherine There is someone there!

Ellen No one at all, you have been dreaming again.

Catherine Don't you see that face? There . . .

Ellen Only the moon on the window, child.

Catherine It is behind there still! And it stirred. Who is it? Oh Nelly, this room is haunted, I'm afraid of being alone.

Ellen You are not alone. I am here. Go to sleep.

Catherine I'm burning, Nelly! I wish I were out of doors—I wish I were a girl again, half savage and free, laughing at injuries not maddening under them. Why am I so changed, Nelly? Why does my blood rush into a hell of tumult at a few words? I know I should be myself, were I once among the heather on those hills—Open the window again—wide—

Ellen And give you your death of cold!

Catherine Give me a chance of life, you mean! (*She darts to the window, throws it open and leans out*) Look, there's my room with the candle in it! See the trees swaying before the window—the other candle is in Joseph's garret; Joseph sits up late, doesn't he? He is waiting till I come home that he may lock the gate. Well, he'll wait a while yet! It's a rough journey and I must pass by Gimmerton Kirk to go that journey! We've braved its ghosts often together and dared each other to stand amongst the graves and ask them to come! Heathcliff! I dare you now! Will you venture? If you do I'll keep you. They may bury me twelve feet deep and throw the church down over me! I won't rest till you are with me, I never will!

Edgar comes in

Ellen Oh sir, my poor mistress—she quite masters me.

Edgar Leave her with me. Catherine?

Ellen Her mind wanders, sir. We must have the doctor—

Edgar closes the window

Catherine Open the window!

Edgar No, my love, it would not be good for you.

Catherine Edgar Linton! You are one of those things that are ever found when least wanted.

Edgar Catherine—

Catherine But you shan't keep me from my narrow home out yonder—my resting place where I'm bound when spring is over.

Edgar Catherine—am I nothing to you any more? Do you love Heath—

Catherine Hush! Mention that name, and I end the matter instantly—

Edgar Catherine—

Catherine What you now hold, you may have—but before you lay hands on me again, my soul will be on that hill-top.

Pause

Ellen Sir—Mr Linton, come. (*She draws him away*) Send for Dr Kenneth as fast as you can. She will be quiet now, she is after an energetic fit ... please go, sir ...

Edgar Catherine, I will leave you and not come again until you ask for me, but you must rest now; Nelly will look after you ...

Catherine gets back on the couch with Ellen's help. There is a slight pause, then:

Edgar exits

Ellen tucks Catherine in, and she sleeps

Ellen exits

There is a pause, then Heathcliff comes from the shadows

Heathcliff approaches Catherine, bends down and gently kisses her. She stirs

Catherine (*whispering*) Heathcliff?

Heathcliff Oh, Cathy!

Catherine Heathcliff, is it you? No dream?

Heathcliff No dream—I've watched all night.

Catherine Heathcliff.

Heathcliff Oh Cathy! Oh, my life! How can I bear it?

Catherine How so? You and Edgar have broken my heart—and now you both bewail the dead to me!

He goes to rise. She holds him

How strong you are! How many years do you mean to live after I have gone?

Heathcliff (*again trying to rise*) Don't torture me—

Catherine I wish I could hold you till we were both dead. Why shouldn't you suffer?—I do!

Heathcliff Cathy—

Catherine Will you forget me? Will you be happy when I am in the earth? Will you say in twenty years time, "That is the grave of Catherine Earnshaw? I loved her once, and was wretched to lose her, but it passed"—will you say so, Heathcliff?

He moves away

Heathcliff You know I could as soon forget you as myself. While you are at peace—

Catherine I shall not be at peace—
Heathcliff I shall writhe in the torments of hell.
Catherine I do not wish you greater torment than I suffer, Heathcliff—I only wish us never to be parted.
Heathcliff We never shall be.

She rises. For a moment they hold apart, then are locked in an embrace

Heathcliff This is the depth of your cruelty. Why did you despise me, Cathy? Why did you betray your own heart?
Catherine (*sobbing*) Let me alone!
Heathcliff I have not broken your heart—*you* have broken it—and in breaking it you have broken mine.
Catherine Let me alone!
Heathcliff So much the worse for me that I am strong!
Catherine If I've done wrong, I'm dying for it. You left me too. I forgive you. Forgive me!
Heathcliff Hard to forgive—to look at those eyes—kiss me. Kiss me but don't let me see your eyes! I forgive you the death you have given me in life.

They kiss, their faces hidden against each others as they weep

Ellen has been present in the shadows for some time

Ellen Quick! Mr Linton is coming!
Heathcliff I must go, Cathy—
Catherine No!
Heathcliff If I live, I'll see you before you are asleep.
Catherine You must not go!
Ellen Miss Cathy!
Heathcliff I'll wait below your window.
Catherine You shall not go, I tell you!
Heathcliff For an hour.
Catherine Not for a minute!
Ellen Don't listen to her!

Heathcliff tries to free himself

Catherine No! Don't go! Don't go! It is the last time!
Ellen Go while you are still safe—
Catherine Edgar will not hurt us—
Ellen Too late—
Catherine Heathcliff, I shall die! I shall die!

Catherine falls limp in Heathcliff's arms as:

Edgar runs in

Edgar springs at the couple. Heathcliff places the lifeless form in Edgar's arms

Heathcliff Help her, before you settle with me.

Heathcliff goes

Edgar slowly carries Catherine from the room

The Lights fade down except on Ellen

Ellen rises and comes forward to speak to Lockwood in the shadows

Ellen The child was born. That Catherine you saw at Wuthering Heights. Two hours later the mother was dead. I don't know if it is a peculiarity in me but I am seldom otherwise than happy when watching in a chamber of death. No angel in heaven could have looked more beautiful than she appeared. To be sure, one may have doubted after the wayward existence she had led, whether she merited a haven of peace at last—but not there—not in the presence of her happy release!

Heathcliff emerges from the shadows

She goes to him

Heathcliff She's dead. I've not waited for you to learn that. Put your handkerchief away—don't snivel before me! Damn you all. She wants none of *your* tears.

Ellen Yes, she is dead. Gone to heaven I hope, where we may, everyone, join her, if we take due warning and leave our evil ways to follow good.

Heathcliff Did *she* take due warning then? Did *she* die like a saint? How did—(*His hand goes to his eyes and he says quietly*) How did she die, Nelly?

Ellen (*taking his other hand in hers*) —Quiet as a lamb—she drew a sigh, and stretched herself, like a child reviving, and sinking again into sleep.

Heathcliff Did she . . . speak of me?

Ellen Her senses never returned. She recognized nobody from the time you left her. She never saw her daughter. Her life closed in a gentle dream—may she wake as kindly in the other world.

Heathcliff May she wake in hell! Liar to the end!

He breaks away from Ellen and with frightful vehemence calls all about him, lit by a single spotlight

> Where are you?
> Not there! Not in heaven!
> Not perished—where?
> You said you cared for nothing for my sufferings!
> And I pray one prayer—
> I repeat it till my tongue stiffens:
> CATHERINE EARNSHAW
> May you not rest as long as I am living!
> If I killed you,
> Haunt me!
> Be with me always; take any form; drive me mad!
> Only do not leave me in this darkness
> Where I cannot find you!

The Light on Heathcliff goes out

Lockwood enters to Ellen

Lockwood And what of his own wife? What of Isabella?

Ellen Isabella bore him a son—and took her own revenge—as he continued to take his.

Lights up on Wuthering Heights

Heathcliff enters with a sheaf of papers, calling Joseph, who appears

Heathcliff Joseph! Tell Hindley to come here.
Joseph He's noan drunk. Tha'll not make much wi' 'im toneeght.
Heathcliff Fetch him here, you clod! Drag him if you must.
Joseph I'll do what I can.
Heathcliff Do as you're bid and do it now!

Joseph exits

Heathcliff glances through the papers and then arranges them in some order on the table. He fetches ink, sand and quills

    Hindley comes on slowly, sober but in a state of great physical degeneration: like a starved and beaten animal but suspicious and on his guard

Heathcliff regards him with satisfaction

    I've never seen you looking better! Where's my slut of a wife?
Hindley Ha!

Hindley smiles and would laugh if Heathcliff's bark didn't divert his slow thought

Heathcliff Quiet, you fool, where is Isabella?
Hindley Gone.
Heathcliff Where? Where is she gone? Tell me!
Hindley (*to Joseph*) Time—? What o'clock is it?
Joseph Nearer nine nor ten.
Hindley Away! You'll never catch her—she's off. London, Bristol, the West Indies—she's out of your way Heathcliff, for good.
Heathcliff It suits me. But the boy—has she taken the boy?
Hindley (*smiling his half-idiot smile again*) Smashed her wedding ring—with poker. There's gold for you there Heathcliff—in the hearth!
Heathcliff The boy? (*To Joseph*) What do you know of this?
Joseph Nay—tha' knows I'm come from Gimmerton—
Hindley Lost him too, Heathcliff. All gone. Her parting words were "Tell him the boy now has a name—Linton." Linton Heathcliff! (*He laughs*)
Heathcliff She wants me to hate the brat too? Linton!! (*He almost spits*) Very well—in my own good time, when I want him—*if* I want him—I'll have him. For now, good riddance. I've business with you.
Hindley I'll do no business now. I'm on my way to meet—
Heathcliff On your way to hell! You wander in your mind. It's a year since you've been out of the house. Do you know what you look like?
Hindley Do I care what I look like? Do you?
Heathcliff Show your face and your own dogs will bark at you! (*He indicates the papers*) I want your assent on these—if your hand is too palsied, I shall guide it.

He thrusts him into a chair by the table

    Sign your name there!
Hindley I'll sign nothing you've had a hand in rigging.

Heathcliff You shall. There. . . .
Hindley Why the devil should I put my name to anything you command?
Heathcliff Until you do I'll keep you under lock and key in the dark; your victuals spig-swill, every bottle and cask in the house will be smashed and let run dry. If needs be I'll see you die with your eyes open and sober!
Hindley I should have broken your back! I'll not sign, I'll not read—nothing to do with deeds and testaments.
Heathcliff The law's with me in this: you owe me more than you can pay. The mortgages are enough but I'll make quite sure—I'll have that document signed. Put your name on that paper.
Hindley (*rising with something of his former self*) I warned you what you'd come to: your time is up. (*He produces the pistol*) I'll send you to hell! I've formed my resolution, by God I'll execute it. (*He moves away from the table*)
Heathcliff Joseph—is that thing loaded?
Hindley Ruined . . . Hareton a pauper . . .
Joseph O Lord, why mun we come to this?
Heathcliff Be still!
Hindley Justice of a sort. Hareton shall know I did for you. Before you go—there's one spot where I can plague you still—Where is Catherine? Wouldn't you like to stretch yourself on her grave and die like a faithful dog? Bastard! I'm glad the thing you prized is dead—carrion! She rots, Heathcliff . . . rots . . .

Heathcliff jumps at him. "He flung himself on Earnshaw's weapon and wrenched it from his grasp. The charge exploded and the knife in springing back closed into its owner's wrist. Heathcliff pulled it away, slitting the flesh, and putting it, dripping, into his pocket. With Hindley on the ground he kicked and trampled him . . . dashed his head against the flags. He exerted preterhuman self-denial in abstaining from finishing him altogether, then dragged the senseless body onto the settle."

Joseph's feeble efforts at interference have been checked by a savage thrust from Heathcliff which knocked him to the ground. He crawls alway

Joseph Ye'll not murder me like ye've done for 'im! I'm off for t' magistrate to inquire into this . . . O Lord . . .
Heathcliff (*dragging him back*) You'll stop here. You know your master's hand.
Joseph (*tending Hindley*) Heathcliff, thy bad . . .
Heathcliff Keep your sermons to yourself. Remember this . . . (*Glancing at Hindley*) I think he'll live. Whether he does or not is no matter. Do you still comprehend me? Mr Hindley. All is *mine*! Hareton—your son—is *mine*! And we'll see if one tree won't grow as crooked as another, with the same wind to twist it! The Guest is now the Master of Wuthering Heights! (*He turns*)
Ellen And in time Thrushcross Grange.

The Lights fade and come up on Ellen and Lockwood

(*Sighing*) Mind you, I don't think he cares a jot for either place. They are just the outward sign that he has conquered. He is indeed Master of Wuthering Heights. And Hareton, who should be the first gentleman of the neighbourhood, is reduced to complete dependence on his father's enemy; he lives in his own house as a servant, deprived of everything and unable to right himself because of his gentle, simple nature and his ignorance that he has been wronged.

Lockwood What intrigued me at the start and what I still don't understand is the presence of young Catherine at the Heights. How did she come under Heathcliff's charge? How came she to marry his son?

Ellen When Isabella died Heathcliff got possession of the boy. Linton was ever a weakling—I never thought to see him reach manhood. My poor master—Edgar Linton—kept little Cathy well away from Wuthering Heights but when he died Heathcliff descended, abducted her and married her to his son, thus securing the inheritance that gave him Thrushcross Grange.

Lockwood But there is law in the land! This is England not some bandit-ridden island! "Abduct" and "marry by force"—it sounds, my dear Mrs Dean, very much like the lurid plot of an opera.

Ellen I don't know how he did it any more than I know how he got his money and style in the years he was away. Young Heathcliff died almost as soon as wed—so you have that pretty kettle of fish up there now. I would do anything to rescue Miss Cathy—she's no more Mrs Heathcliff than I am. I once thought I would take a cottage, and get her to come and live with me. But Mr Heathcliff would as soon permit that as he would set up Hareton in an independent house. (*Rising and moving off*) I must see to your supper. If you go up to the Heights again sir, take her a note from me.

Lockwood (*to the audience as at the opening of the play*) I delivered Mrs Dean's note to Wuthering Heights, at the same time giving Mr Heathcliff notice that he should should look for another tenant for Thrushcross Grange. I felt no disposition to pass another winter there. (*He turns—then turns back*) In the September of the next year, on my way to visit a friend in the north, I found myself within fifteen miles of Gimmerton, and I acted on a sudden impulse to break my journey, see whether another tenant had been found, and settle matters finally with my landlord. I walked down through the valley. The grey church looked greyer, and the lonely churchyard lonelier: a moor sheep was cropping the short turf on the graves. I climbed up to Wuthering Heights. I had neither to climb the gate, nor to knock—it yielded to my hand. This is an improvement, I thought. The air was heavy with the fragrance of stocks and wallflowers . . . all the doors and lattices were open—and in the kitchen . . .

Evening birdsong. The sound of singing and laughter

Lockwood stands on the outskirts, as the lights come up on Wuthering Heights, which glows warm and homely

Ellen sits at the hearth sewing. On the settle sit Hareton and Cathy, reading

Cathy "Contrary." "Contrary." That's the third time you've got it wrong, you dunce! I won't tell you again!

Hareton I forgot—

Cathy Well—remember, or I'll pull your hair!

Hareton "Contrary."

Cathy That's right!

Hareton Now kiss me for remembering.

Cathy Not until you read it all over first correctly—without a single mistake, mind!

Hareton Mary, Mary, quite contrary, how does your garden grow. (*Giggling, he reads it to her, with many a kiss*)

Ellen smiles at them, and sings to herself

Joseph enters, grumbling, with logs for the fire

Joseph Aw'd rather hev 'em swearing i' my lugs frough morn tuh neeght, than hearken tuh yuh row! But yah're a raught nowt, Nelly Dean, un' she's another, un' that poor lad 'ull be lost atween ye. Poor lad! Ye've witched him—oh Lord, judge 'em.

Ellen Oh shut your row, old man, and go and read your Bible!

They laugh as Joseph goes out grumbling

Ellen sees Lockwood standing in the shadows and crosses to him

Who is there?

Lockwood It is only I, Mrs Dean.

Ellen Why Mr Lockwood! You should have given us notice, we—

Lockwood Hush—a short visit only.

Hareton You are welcome, sir.

Cathy Aye, welcome.

Lockwood I thank you.

Ellen We were not expecting you.

Lockwood I beg you—be easy.

He draws Ellen aside

Hareton and Cathy return to their occupation

Lockwood There is much here that I was not expecting.

Ellen (*looking back*) Within a fortnight of your leaving us—perhaps it was the note you brought from me—I was summoned to Wuthering Heights, to look after the house—and Miss Cathy. And as winter grew into spring, she grew restless at her isolation and confinement, turned more and more to her cousin, held out the hand of friendship—and as spring grew into summer—Oh, it has not been easy—he was not to be civilized with a wish, and she is no paragon of patience—and Joseph was aghast to see his favourite change sides—but both are tending to the same point— the crown of all my wishes. And then I tell you, sir, there won't be a happier woman in all England.

Lockwood But how does Heathcliff—

Ellen Heathcliff? Then you have not heard?

Lockwood Heard what?

Ellen As winter grew into spring, and spring into summer—

The Lights fade down

Heathcliff enters as we saw him in the first act, a candle in his hand, searching about him

Heathcliff   Catherine! Cathy!
I am weary of waiting.
Now it is in my power to destroy both our houses, I have lost the will.
I cannot bear to look at her
But in Hareton's face I see the ghost of my immortal love. My pride,
my happiness, my anguish—

Cathy!
I grow weary of the days of living—
I am animated with hunger and seemingly I must not eat
I have to remind myself to breathe
Almost remind my heart to beat.
Why don't you come?
For there is a strange change approaching—
At present I am but in its shadow.
With my bare hands I opened your grave
The side of your coffin ready for me
I know you are there and not there
I heard your voice once in the air
Above me!
Speak again!
Speak again!
O God! It is a long fight, and I wish it were over!

It seems suddenly as if the whole room is full of unseen presences: sounds that might be half-articulated thoughts; a restless fluttering something which may be only in Heathcliff's mind, something that tells him the moment of change has come

In the flutter of sound, Catherine's voice

Catherine Let me in! Let me in! Heathcliff . . .
Heathcliff   Cathy!
Come in, come in!
Cathy, do come, oh do come once more!
My heart's true love, hear me this time . . .
Catherine, at last!

He moves into the darkness. Sudden complete silence

Ellen The lattice flapped to and fro, grazing his hand that lay stretched through the window—but no blood trickled from the broken skin.

Joseph enters

Joseph Th' divil's harried off 'is soul—an' 'e can 'av his carcase into the bargain for all I care!
Ellen His face was washed with rain.
Joseph Ech! What a wicked 'un 'e looks, grinning at death!
Ellen I could not close his eyes.
Joseph (*moving off*) I thank thee, Lord, who in Thy Mercy hast restored this house to its lawful Masters . . .

His voice fades with the Lights

Ellen walks to the extreme left, meeting Lockwood. They stroll across the front of the stage and eventually she precedes him off

Ellen To the scandal of the whole district we buried him as he wished—in Catherine's grave and no service.
Lockwood And what will become of Wuthering Heights?

Ellen When Cathy and Hareton marry, they will live at the Grange.
Lockwood And Wuthering Heights?
Ellen Closed.
Lockwood For the use of such ghosts as care to inhabit it?
Ellen No, Mr Lockwood. I believe the dead are at peace.

Ellen exits

Lockwood On my way home, I went to the kirkyard on the edge of the moor; Hindley, Linton, Edgar, Catherine, Heathcliff. Already the heath and the bilberries and the turf and moss creep over them and they will soon be covered. The country people who had a lively fear of Heathcliff swear on their Bibles that he *walks*. I lingered there, under that benign sky: watched the moths fluttering among the heath and harebells; listened to the soft wind breathing through the grass. And I wondered how anyone could ever imagine unquiet slumbers for the sleepers in that quiet earth.

The Light fades

CURTAIN

FURNITURE AND PROPERTY LIST

A composite set comprising three main areas; the kitchen of Wuthering Heights; a room at Thrushcross Grange; Ellen Dean's "corner". Between these areas; dark, undefined spaces.

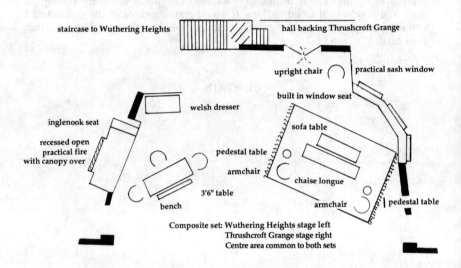

staircase to Wuthering Heights   hall backing Thrushcroft Grange

upright chair   practical sash window

built in window seat

welsh dresser

inglenook seat   sofa table

recessed open
practical fire
with canopy over   pedestal table

armchair   chaise longue

3'6" table

bench   armchair   pedestal table

Composite set: Wuthering Heights stage left
Thrushcroft Grange stage right
Centre area common to both sets

ACT I

On stage: **Wuthering Heights kitchen**
Fire enclosure with an "open fire" and high mantel. Stone inscription above
On the mantel: tea-caddy, lighted candle, mirror, large book
In the fire enclosure: tea-making implements (kettle, teapot, etc.)
settle
Dresser with bowls, plates, etc, *Inside it:* bread, brandy bottle, glass
Table Two chairs
Calendar on wall
Two chairs
Table. *On it:* sewing

Thrushcross Grange
Large window enclosure with window which opens
Door with key in lock
Couch
"Open" fire. *By it:* fire-irons
Two small tables. *On one:* a book
Sofa
Knitting or sewing: baby-clothes
Two small chairs

Off stage: Storm-lantern, alight **(Joseph)**
Duster **(Ellen)**
Horse-whip **(Hindley)**
Cradle. *In it:* a "baby" **(Ellen)**

Personal: **Ellen:** chatelaine with keys (*required throughout*)

ACT II

Strike: *Wuthering Heights*
Mirror
Calendar
Cradle

Set: *Wuthering Heights*
In dresser: ink, sand, quills

Off stage: Tea-tray with tea, etc. **(Ellen)**
Pillow with feathers escaping **(Catherine)**
Bedding for the couch **(Ellen)**
Sheaf of papers **(Heathcliff)**
Book **(Cathy** and **Hareton)**
Sewing **(Ellen)**
Logs for fire **(Joseph)**
Lighted candle **(Heathcliff)**

Personal: **Hindley:** pistol with double-edged spring knife attached to barrel (*required throughout Act II*)

LIGHTING PLOT

Fittings required "open" fires at both Wuthering Heights and Thrushcross Grange

ACT I

To open: Curtain rises on a completely dark stage; pinspot on **Lockwood**

Cue 1	**Lockwood** goes off *Lights up slowly on kitchen, leaving rest of stage in darkness; a blazing fire in the open fireplace*	(Page 1)
Cue 2	**Joseph:** ". . . 'cos 'e's comin'—eh!' *Very dim light on Heathcliff descending back stairs*	(Page 4)
Cue 3	**Heathcliff** sits on settle and closes his eyes *Lights fade to dark*	(Page 8)
Cue 4	**Heathcliff:** "Who is that?" **Lockwood** runs downstairs *Lights up slightly*	(Page 8)
Cue 5	**Lockwood**, on his way out, looks back at **Heathcliff** *Lights down, remaining only on* **Heathcliff**	(Page 10)
Cue 6	**Heathcliff:** "Catherine! . . ." *Lights fade on* **Heathcliff**, *the come up on* **Ellen**	(Page 10)
Cue 7	**Ellen** ". . . that things began to change . . ." *Daylight builds in room at Wuthering Heights*	(Page 11)
Cue 8	**Edgar:** leads **Catherine** off *Lights check down*	(Page 16)
Cue 9	**Ellen:** ". . . and in such days . . ." *Lights up full*	(Page 26)
Cue 10	**Hindley** exits. **Catherine** and **Edgar** embrace *Fade lights slowly except on* **Ellen** *and* **Lockwood**	(Page 27)

ACT II

To open: Curtain up on summer "evening" light

Cue 11	**Catherine:** "I'll be back again directly." She goes *Lights progressively darker outside; firelight begins to take effect*	(Page 29)
Cue 12	**Ellen** exits *"Sunlight" illuminates* **Isabella** *as she walks to the window*	(Page 34)
Cue 13	**Catherine** backs away *Lights fade*	(Page 40)
Cue 14	**Ellen:** ". . . long-meditated plan of revenge." *Lights up on Wuthering Heights*	(Page 40)

Cue 15	**Isabella** and **Joseph** struggle with Hindley and get him behind the settle *Lights fade*	(Page 43)
Cue 16	**Heathcliff** exits *Lights up on Catherine*	(Page 43)
Cue 17	**Edgar** carries **Catherine** from the room *Lights gradually fade down except on* **Ellen**	(Page 47)
Cue 18	**Heathcliff** "Liar to the end!" *Single spot on Heathcliff*	(Page 47)
Cue 19	**Heathcliff:** "Where I cannot find you!" *Light out on Heathcliff*	(Page 47)
Cue 20	**Ellen:** ". . . as he continued to take his." *Lights up on Wuthering Heights*	(Page 47)
Cue 21	**Ellen:** "And in time Thrushcross Grange." *Lights fade and come up on Ellen and Lockwood*	(Page 49)
Cue 22	Evening birdsong, sound of singing and laughter *Lights up on Wuthering Heights, a warm and homely glow*	(Page 50)
Cue 23	**Ellen:** ". . . and spring into summer –" *Lights fade*	(Page 51)
Cue 24	**Joseph:** "Thy Mercy hast restored this home to its lawful masters . . ." *Lights fade*	(Page 52)
Cue 25	**Lockwood:** ". . . for the sleepers in that quiet earth." *Light fades*	(Page 53)

EFFECTS PLOT

ACT I

Cue 1   Lights up on Wuthering Heights kitchen   (Page 1)
Doorbell rings; then loud knocking and dogs barking

Cue 2   **Joseph** goes off   (Page 1)
Sound of door being opened, chains, bolts, etc.

Cue 3   **Lockwood** snatches lantern from **Joseph** and runs off   (Page 7)
Sound of door crashing open and immediate uproar from dogs

Cue 4   Lights fade to dark on scene, but light still on **Heathcliff**   (Page 8)
Low moan of wind; clock chimes a quarter hour

Cue 5   **Heathcliff:** "Catherine! ..."   (Page 10)
Breeze blows

Cue 6   **Catherine:** "... for anything you do for that matter."   (Page 14)
Sound of horses' hooves on flagstones outside

Cue 7   **Catherine:** "... who know nothing and say nothing!"   (Page 14)
Sound of footsteps

Cue 8   **Ellen** goes off   (Page 16)
Sound of door being bolted

Cue 9   **Ellen:** "For shame!"   (Page 17)
A crash off stage

Cue 10   **Catherine:** "... but as my own being!"   (Page 23)
A mighty thunderclap

Cue 11   **Ellen** goes off   (Page 23)
Thunder

Cue 13   **Joseph** goes off   (Page 23)
Thunder

Cue 13   **Catherine** tries to run out; **Ellen** drags her back   (Page 23)
Thunder

Cue 14   **Ellen:** "... I'll ferret Master Heathcliff out!"   (Page 24)
Thunder

Cue 15   **Catherine** runs out   (Page 24)
Massive clap of thunder, heavy rain; great wind rises

Cue 16   **Joseph:** "... Strike 'em!"   (Page 24)
Loudest thunder-crash; sound of brickwork crashing down

ACT II

Cue 17   **Ellen** opens the window   (Page 44)
          Wind blasts in

Cue 18   **Lockwood:** "... all the doors and lattices were open—and in the   (Page 50)
          kitchen—"
          Evening birdsong, sound of singing and laughter

Cue 19   **Heathcliff:** "... It is a long fight, and I wish it were over."   (Page 52)
          The "room" is filled with unseen presences: flutterings, whisperings, etc.

Cue 20   **Heathcliff:** "... Catherine at last." He moves into the darkness   (Page 52)
          Cut all effects: sudden complete silence

          Curtain

MADE AND PRINTED IN GREAT BRITAIN BY
LATIMER TREND & COMPANY LTD PLYMOUTH

MADE IN ENGLAND